A LIVELIHOOD FROM

A Livelihood from Fishing

Globalization and sustainable fisheries policies

Compiled by ALAIN LE SANN

Intermediate Technology Publications 1998

Intermediate Technology Publications
103–105 Southampton Row, London WC1B 4HH, UK

This is an expanded edition of *Pêcher pour vivre*, published in France in 1995

A CIP catalogue record for this book is available from the British Library

ISBN 1 85339 398 3

Typeset by J&L Composition Ltd, Filey, North Yorkshire
Printed in the UK by SRP Exeter

A note on the origins of this book

Pêche et Développement (Fishing and Development) was set up in 1986 as a working group by the French non-governmental organization, Solagral, and became an independent organization in 1995. It comprises teachers, researchers and professionals from the fishing and aquaculture industries, as well as members of non-governmental organizations (NGOs).

The organization works to defend the interests of men and women fishworkers around the world, while also seeking to support ecologists in their efforts to protect oceans and coastal environments. Since 1987, *Pêche et Développement*'s quarterly review has published articles on problems facing the fishing industry not only in France and the rest of Europe, but worldwide.

Another organization, CRISLA (*Centre de Réflexion, d'Information et de Solidarité avec les peuples d'Afrique, d'Asie et d'Amerique Latine*), was founded in 1976 in the town of Lorient, the second largest fishing port in France, with the objective of 'decolonizing' the North's view of Southern countries. CRISLA seeks to encourage reflection on the relationship between North and South and to demonstrate that, if solidarity is to be achieved, the North must change its outlook.

CRISLA publishes the *Pêche et Développement* quarterly bulletin. In 1992 it published *Quand reverdiront les villages*, a French translation of the book *Towards Green Villages* by the Indian environmental campaigners, Anil Agarwal and Sunita Narain.

Note The book contains many technical terms which are defined or explained in the Glossary.

Editorial co-ordination: Alain Le Sann

Contributions from: Didier Cadio, Joël Le Bail, Philippe Favrelière and Mustapha Ould El Kettab, Charles Menzies, K.G. Kumar, Brian O'Riordan.

Thanks also to: Jean and Jean-François Breurec, Jean Dréano, Odile Schmitt, Annette Le Zause, Claude Teilhat, Véronique Toulliou and Isabelle Gouville, Gildas le Bïhan.

Illustrations: Gwendal Le Bayon, formatted for this edition by Richard Inglis.

Translated by: Phelipa Seguineau.

Polished and adapted by: K.G. Kumar, Brian O'Riordan and James Smith.

Contents

Foreword

More than a decade on from the 1984 Food and Agriculture Organization (FAO) World Conference on Fisheries Management and Development, the fisheries sector is in a state of crisis characterized by violent clashes on land and at sea, which have escalated to include many other interest groups. Environmental organizations, political parties, journalists and consumer and other pressure groups have now entered the fray. It has been a decade during which the United Nations made a resolution to ban drift-nets on the high seas, the Canadians set gunboats on Spanish fishing vessels in international waters, and the USA and Mexico declared a trade war over a US tuna import embargo. Fish stocks have been overexploited in oceans all over the world, and the human race is confronted, for the first time ever, with the real possibility of the commercial extinction of many of its fish stocks. This poses an immediate challenge for the sector itself. It must formulate innovative development policies for the short and long terms.

The past ten years have also seen the consolidation and spread of fishworkers' organizations to numerous countries. These organizations have increasingly participated in the debate on the crisis in the world's fisheries. While fishery-related negotiations still occur mainly at the national level, three other levels are growing in importance.

The first of these is the local level. It is only here that the foundations can be laid for active participation by fishworkers in managing fish stocks and in ensuring their commitment to ecological issues.

The second is the regional and continental level. From Africa to Europe, fishworkers' movements must keep abreast of political and economic developments (such as the proliferation of free trade zones, for example) and also the burgeoning effects of the expanding fishing industry.

Finally, at the international level, numerous decisions are currently made by international organizations – the prohibition of drift-nets is an example. Hence, the presence of fishworkers in such international contexts is vital to ensure proper representation of their interests.

This book, which essentially sets out to inform readers of these issues, is inspired by Rudolph Strahm's *Pourquoi sont-ils si pauvres?* (published by La Baconnière in 1986) and Bertrand Delpeuch's *L'enjeu alimentaire Nord-Sud* (published by Syros in 1990). We hope that it will lead to a better understanding of the many issues involved in the global fishing industry, that it will encourage solidarity among fishworkers' organizations, and that it will stimulate a continuing dialogue between fishworkers and environmentalists.

Alain Le Sann

Preface

The period of the last five decades has been characterized by staggering technological and social progress for mankind. Nonetheless, the irrefutable fact is that the world is in a sorry state. Human misery and hunger, which should have been abolished in this modern era of medical advancement, have only spread to affect more and more of the world's populations.

It is in this context that the issue of how oceans ought to feature as a source of food for mankind assumes importance. Will mankind be looking seawards to solve the food security problems of the twenty-first century? The question is particularly relevant since nutritional needs are set to grow along with the world population, which is estimated at six billion in 2000, and predicted to pass nine billion in 2050. Furthermore, agricultural production will almost certainly reach a plateau or even decline, as a result of deterioration of the soil and continuing deforestation all around the world.

There is an enormous discrepancy between the North and the South in the consumption of seafood – 27 kg per person per year in the North, compared to 9 kg per person per year in the South. This cannot be explained solely by the superior biological fertility of coastal waters off developed countries. The discrepancy, as the authors of this book argue, is, above all, due to the fact that the underdevelopment and indebtedness of Southern countries oblige them to forego part of their own fish supply.

While, overall, production from fisheries and aquaculture has grown enormously over recent years in the South, the produce has increasingly been exported to earn foreign currency. The net result is that supplies have gone to the more industrialized regions of the world, where demand is continually on the rise. They have not gone to serve the nutritional needs of local populations. In other words, ocean resources are benefiting populations which already enjoy high levels of food intake, rather than those which are short of protein.

Simultaneously, another anomaly can be observed – the mismanagement of fisheries resources, including fish, molluscs and shellfish, whose nutritional value is unanimously acknowledged. It is an unpalatable and immoral fact that a third of all fish catches (about 30 million tonnes) is destined not to feed humans, but to fatten livestock (poultry, cattle, pigs, salmon, shrimps, and so on). Not only is this utterly wasteful, it is biologically nonsensical.

Similarly absurd is the fact that tens of millions of tonnes of fish and other marine animals are thrown back into the sea from fishing vessels just because nothing has been done to sell them. Hundreds of shrimp trawlers work to supply the dining tables of a few rich countries while, out at sea, other fish (the so-called by-catches) are discarded just a few miles away from the African or Asian coasts. At the same time nearly one billion men, women and children struggle on in poverty and hunger . . . .

What about aquaculture, often billed the great hope for aqua-production of the future? This topic is given ample consideration in this book for a very good reason – over the next 20 or 30 years, aquaculture production is predicted to grow to the same level as current production from capture fisheries. Can aquaculture really provide an alternative to wild, capture fishery? We believe that it can, but only if due respect is paid to nature and to the environment. Ominously enough, spurred by speculative interests, most intensive aquaculture units are concentrating on high-value species, such as salmon and shrimps, rather than on producing food to supply those in need. These units simultaneously pose a threat to the biological fertility and quality of the neighbouring environment and coastal waters.

The only sensible way forward is through extensive or perhaps semi-extensive aquaculture, i.e. only systems sensitive to fragile ecosystems. A reduction of investment at all levels is required. Its socio-economic viability has been clearly demonstrated by China, where for centuries the culture of freshwater fish has been successfully integrated into agricultural systems in combination with, for example, pig rearing or rice cultivation.

Ultimately, effective management of the oceans' resources will depend on our ability to organize its exploitation in the interests and benefit of each and every stakeholder. Classical fishing development strategies, conceived by research bodies and implemented by governments, rarely achieve their objectives. The harsh reality of competition and the yearning for quick, short-term gains inevitably make us continue to behave as though fish stocks and ocean resources were inexhaustible. With advanced methods of capture, mankind has become an even more formidable predator. Our assaults on the hydrosphere have become veritable raids on the world's precious fish stocks. No wonder our seas are overfished – this is the logical outcome of a system which drives ship-owners to intensify their fishing effort and to extend their areas of operation without any regard for the medium- or long-term effects on the marine ecosystem.

Clearly, as the authors of this book exhort, codes of good practice which will help define responsible fishing techniques and processes are long overdue. Without such codes, we will continue to endanger our own prospects for survival. Substitute selfishness with solidarity, and short-term carelessness with thoughtful deliberation – that should be the message for the twenty-first century.

Happily, it is precisely such a message that this book conveys. Designed to unveil the issues in an accessible manner, it draws upon numerous examples to try and answer some of the vexatious questions plaguing the world's fisheries. The oceans and their marine wealth comprise a vulnerable living resource which, as this book powerfully argues, needs to be protected from wastage and greed.

Jean Chaussade
Director of Research
CNRS, University of Nantes

SECTION 1
FISHERIES TODAY

A valuable source of protein

Fish consumption 1987 - 89 by region and in selected countries as a percentage of total animal protein consumption

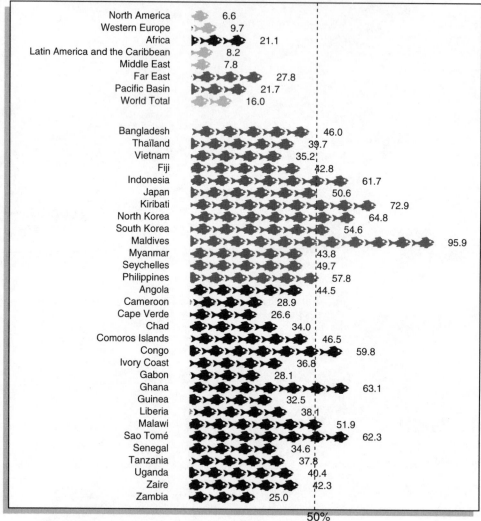

North America	6.6
Western Europe	9.7
Africa	21.1
Latin America and the Caribbean	8.2
Middle East	7.8
Far East	27.8
Pacific Basin	21.7
World Total	16.0
Bangladesh	46.0
Thaïland	39.7
Vietnam	35.2
Fiji	42.8
Indonesia	61.7
Japan	50.6
Kiribati	72.9
North Korea	64.8
South Korea	54.6
Maldives	95.9
Myanmar	43.8
Seychelles	49.7
Philippines	57.8
Angola	44.5
Cameroon	28.9
Cape Verde	26.6
Chad	34.0
Comoros Islands	46.5
Congo	59.8
Ivory Coast	36.8
Gabon	28.1
Ghana	63.1
Guinea	32.5
Liberia	38.1
Malawi	51.9
Sao Tomé	62.3
Senegal	34.6
Tanzania	37.8
Uganda	40.4
Zaire	42.3
Zambia	25.0

50%

Africa

Asia

Other

Source : FAO

© A Le Sann – CRISLA, 1995

Fish is an essential food

All over the world, fish plays a vital role in feeding millions of people. In 1994, the average per capita availability of fish was only 13.6 kg per person per year. In some populations, the average consumption is already much higher. In countries of the Southern hemisphere, the consumption is 9 kg per person per year, a third of the developed countries' level of 27 kg per person per year.

Nonetheless, in most Asian and African countries, fish is a major food item, representing, respectively, 29 per cent and 25 per cent of the supply of animal protein in local diets. In certain landlocked African countries endowed with lakes, such as Chad, Uganda and Zaire, fish accounts for 30–40 per cent of the protein intake. Of the 40 countries scattered across the globe where fish is the principal source of protein, 39 are in the South.

As food, fish is particularly healthy and nutritious. Quite apart from its calorific value, it is a source of easily digestible, high-quality protein. Rich in amino acids, fish also contains calcium, phosphorus, iron, and vitamins A and D. It can enhance the diet of poor populations, where cereals and root vegetables or tubers comprise the staple food. As a supplement, fish thus helps prevent diseases associated with nutritional imbalances. Moreover, fish is relatively inexpensive. In Africa and Asia, fish often costs less than meat. At the fish auction in Abidjan, Ivory Coast, for instance, prices range from 130 CFA francs per kilogram for sardines to 250 CFA francs for threadfin, while prices for meat range from 250 to 1000 CFA francs (see *Conserver et transformer le poisson*, CTA-GRET, 1993).

Unfortunately, in the poorest countries, domestic consumption of marine produce is often hampered by the bias towards exports of fish products from South to North, as well as by the demographic growth.

Worldwide, fish constitutes the principal source of animal protein: 70 million tonnes are directly consumed by man. This figure is higher than the figures for pork (60 million tonnes), beef (50 million tonnes) and poultry (32 million tonnes).

In Asia, one billion people depend on fish and other marine produce as the source of their animal protein. Sixty per cent of populations in the South obtain 40 per cent of their animal protein intake from fish.

Source: *The End of Fish*, Greenpeace, 1994.

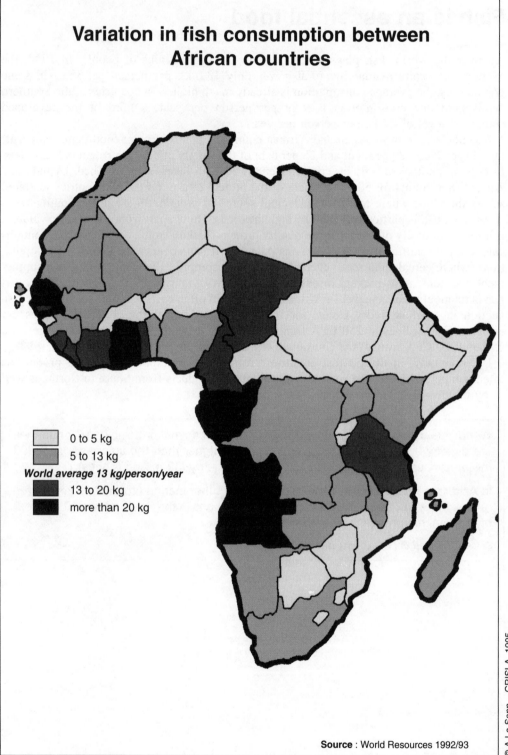

Variation in fish consumption between African countries

0 to 5 kg
5 to 13 kg
World average 13 kg/person/year
13 to 20 kg
more than 20 kg

Source : World Resources 1992/93

© A Le Sann – CRISLA, 1995

Consumption levels are unequal

The Food and Agriculture Organization (FAO) estimates that, in 1994, the global average fish consumption was 13.6 kg per person per year. But behind this figure lies a wide variation. Developed countries consume much more than so-called Third World countries – 27 kg per person per year, compared with 9 kg per person per year. The disparity is even starker if regional averages are compared. Japan, as a major fish consuming country, has a per capita fish consumption of over 70 kg per person per year, while in Iceland the per capita availability of fish is 90 kg per annum. By contrast, per capita fish consumption in Eastern Europe is very low: below 10 kg. In the South consumption figures are close to average. Consumption in South-east Asia and Latin America, at 9 kg per person per year, is only marginally higher than in sub-Saharan Africa, estimated at 7 kg per person per year.

Closer scrutiny at the national level reveals other disparities. The consumption figures for South Korea (52 kg per person per year), the Congo (35 kg per person per year) or the Philippines (34 kg per person per year) are all way above the average for the South. In the same way Iceland is way above average for countries in the North. At the other end of the scale, a resident of Guinea Bissau consumes only 3 kg per year, and in Germany or the Netherlands consumption is only 14 kg per person per year. Following the collapse of the former Soviet Union, per capita fish consumption in the Russian federation has slumped from 29 kg in 1989 to 9 kg in 1993. An important reason for this is the reduction in distant water activities.

Consumption of fish varies with a multitude of factors, such as the scale of production, price, branding and life-styles, among others. Nevertheless, the global demand for fish and marine products continues to grow steadily. This inevitably results in increased fishing effort.

Average fish consumption in Africa is between 5.5 and 8.5 kg per person per year. It varies between 44 kg per person per year in the Congo, and 3 kg per person per year in Guinea Bissau. In Senegal, consumption is 26 kg per person per year and it is nearly 70 kg per person per year in Dakar. In rural areas, consumption is noticeably lower than the national average.

Source: *Conserver et transformer le poisson*, CTA-GRET, 1993.

Estimated consumption of marine produce (1990, kg/person/year)

World average: 13 kg

The North: 27 kg	The South: 9 kg
Japan = 72 kg	Asia = 9.4 kg
Former USSR = 29 kg (10.3 kg in 1995)	Latin America = 8.5 kg
Eastern Europe = 9.6 kg	Africa = 8.5 kg
EU = 22 kg	
North America = 21.6 kg	
Developed Oceania = 20.4 kg	

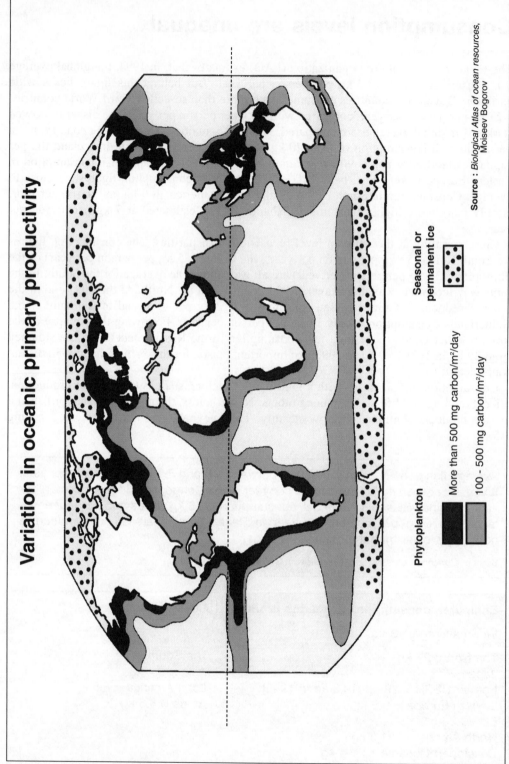

Variation in oceanic primary productivity

Phytoplankton

More than 500 mg carbon/m²/day

100 - 500 mg carbon/m²/day

Seasonal or permanent ice

Source : Biological Atlas of ocean resources,
Moiseev Bogorov

© A Le Sann – CRISLA, 1995

The productivity of oceans varies

While the size of the oceans may give the impression of unlimited resource wealth, more than 90 per cent of the marine fish catch actually comes from only 10 per cent of the oceans – the continental shelf areas (9.9 per cent) and the upwelling zones (0.1 per cent) which tend to occur at the edge of the continental shelf.

As the marine biological cycle requires four elements – light, carbon dioxide, oxygen and nutrient salts – and since these occur in greater abundance over the continental shelf, most of the world's fishing takes place in these areas. Thus, countries which have the widest expanse of continental shelf enjoy a considerable advantage.

By contrast, the fishery productivity of the open oceans has been compared to that of deserts. This is a misleading concept, as the energy and production of the open oceans drive fisheries production. It is the ocean currents that bring nutrient-rich waters from the depths to the surface, producing an abundance of phytoplankton which provide food for many species of fish at the bottom of the food chain. These so-called upwelling zones are associated with some of the richest fishing grounds in the world. However, each species, whether benthic, demersal or pelagic, has its own specific environmental requirements in terms of depth, salinity, temperature and sea bed characteristics.

Fisheries production depends not only on the availability of the four key elements described above, but also on the presence of key habitats in the near-shore waters, in the inter-tidal zone, and in the land areas immediately adjacent to the coast. About two-thirds of all commercially valuable fish species spend the first – and most vulnerable – stages of their life in these waters. However, production is not uniform throughout the coastal area, but is associated with specific habitats and ecosystems. These are highly productive and diverse, which include coastal rivers, bays, wetlands, estuaries, mangroves, saltmarshes, mudflats, sea grass and seaweed beds, and coral reefs.

The temperate waters of the Northern hemisphere appear to be the most productive. The continental shelves here are wider and seasonal water temperature fluctuations ensure a good mixing of water. In warmer and colder regions, where layers of water remain at constant temperatures, the replenishment of nutrient salts is impeded. Nevertheless, tropical and equatorial waters can prove exceptionally productive when upwellings convey with them nutrient salts from below. This happens off the coast of California, Peru, Chile, South and West Africa, Somalia, and the Arabian peninsula.

There are also other qualitative differences between tropical and temperate marine zones. In the sea, as on land, the closer one gets to the equator – from either pole – the greater the species diversity in any given ecosystem. But population size of each species reduces. Thus in the tropical zone there are large numbers of species occurring in relatively small quantities, while in the temperate zones there are small numbers of species occurring in relatively large quantities. This is of crucial importance, though often ignored, in adopting different approaches to fisheries development and management in tropical and temperate fisheries.

Ecuador

Production for export

Catches compared to exports

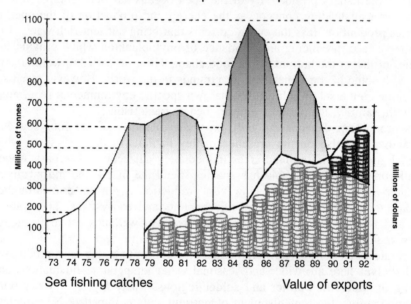

Sea fishing catches   Value of exports

Destinations of catches
1989 - 90 averages

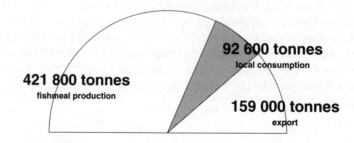

92 600 tonnes
local consumption

421 800 tonnes
fishmeal production

159 000 tonnes
export

Source : FAO

© A Le Sann – CRISLA, 1995

Increasing production is not enough

The people of the Southern hemisphere consume a lot less fish than those in developed countries, but this does not mean that fisheries or fishing techniques are underdeveloped in the South.

While the quantity of fish caught per person is lower in the South (13.5 kg per person per year) than in the North (36 kg per person per year), many Southern countries export much of their catch or transform a major part of it into fishmeal. Thus, local markets and the people of these countries are effectively deprived of this precious protein.

Consider the case of Ecuador. The major part of Ecuadorean fish production (as much as 95 per cent of the catch, notably pilchards, tuna and prawns) is the result of industrial fishing effort and is meant for export. Artisanal fishermen alone supply home markets, but the economic importance of small-scale fishing and its contribution to local social and economic development generally goes unrecognized. More often than not, modernization is equated with industrialization, while the small-scale and artisanal sectors are viewed as obsolete and impervious to change. As a result, this sector finds it nearly impossible to obtain technical, financial or scientific aid from the state.

Of Ecuador's total fish production (672 330 tonnes annually, on average, between 1984 and 1993), the domestic market is supplied with only 13.8 per cent. Over 400 000 tonnes are transformed into fishmeal and 159 000 tonnes exported, while the annual consumption of an Ecuadorean remains under 9 kg.

Evidently, satisfying local food requirements is not a priority. Rather, the priority use of Ecuadorean marine biological resources is to earn foreign currency. The irony is that, despite the potential availability of adequate food supplies from the sea, a large proportion of the population suffers from malnutrition, particularly from a lack of protein. Nearly 200 000 children under five years of age are undernourished, and 46 per cent of pregnant women suffer from anaemia. This plight is caused not only by the inequitable distribution of income, but also by the country's economic choices, such as the decision to give priority to the export of marine produce.

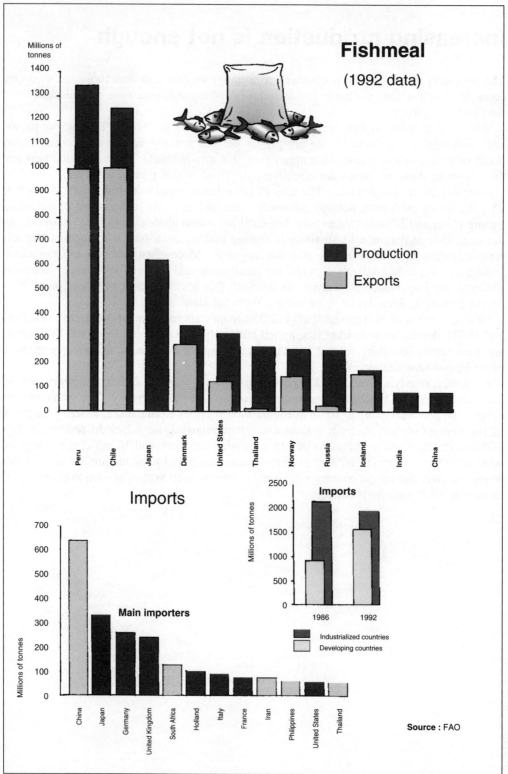

Millions of tonnes

Fishmeal
(1992 data)

Production

Exports

Peru · Chile · Japan · Denmark · United States · Thailand · Norway · Russia · Iceland · India · China

Imports

Millions of tonnes

Main importers

China · Japan · Germany · United Kingdom · South Africa · Holland · Italy · France · Iran · Philippines · United States · Thailand

Imports

Millions of tonnes

1986   1992

Industrialized countries
Developing countries

Source : FAO

Fish is fed to livestock

About a third of global fish production – almost 30 million tonnes – is transformed into fishmeal and into oil. This type of production began around the turn of the century in Scandinavian countries, where oil was produced for human consumption and fishmeal as animal feed. Subsequent technical advances, such as fish detection devices (echo sounders, etc.) and more efficient purse seines, occurred along with a boom in demand from the agriculture sector (where intensive pig and poultry farms are large consumers of fishmeal). This led to a sharp rise in industrial fishing, which targets almost exclusively small fish species like anchovies, sardines and horse mackerel.

The transformation of fish into fishmeal results in an enormous wastage of protein – around five tonnes of fish are used to produce just a single tonne of fishmeal. Moreover, when fishmeal is consumed by poultry, cattle, fish or shellfish (in aquaculture), a further loss of protein occurs. On average, 15 kg of fish are needed to manufacture 2.7 kg of fishmeal. This, in turn, becomes one element in the total feed mix, and contributes to the production of a salmon weighing 3 kg.

Over half the world's fishmeal comes from Peru, Chile and Japan. Yet, industrial fishing represents a substantial proportion of the fishing activities of several other nations. Southern countries supply half the world's fishmeal and are responsible for 70 per cent of its international trade. A substantial share of the marine biological resources of developing countries thus supplies the intensive agriculture production systems of industrialized countries.

Meanwhile, some countries of the South, notably in Asia, have lately begun to require fishmeal to supply their own growing numbers of fish and shrimp farms. With the development of this type of aquaculture, the South has been importing more fishmeal in recent years, while imports into Northern countries have remained stable.

Fishmeal production developed rapidly during the 1980s, then stabilized after 1989, a record year. The production for 1992 of six million tonnes was lower than even that of 1984. However, in 1994 increased catches of anchovy in South America, amounting to some 10 per cent of the global fish catch, led to a corresponding rise in fishmeal production, with nearly 35 million tonnes of fish processed in this way.

Japan
Crisis in the fishing industry

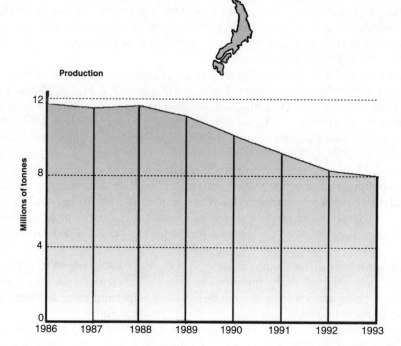

Production

Millions of tonnes

12

8

4

0

1986   1987   1988   1989   1990   1991   1992   1993

Imports

Millions of dollars

13

11

9

7

5

3

1
0

1983 1984 1985 1986 1987 1988 1989 1990 1991 1992

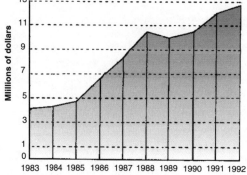

Income from fishing and aquaculture as a proportion of total revenue to fishermen's households

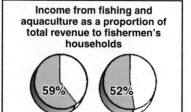

59%   52%

1975   1989

Source : FAO and Fishery Economy Survey

Japan is now a shaky giant

For a long time, Japan was regarded as the undisputed leader of the world's fishing industry, but today it finds itself reduced to a position of vulnerability. Although still a major fish producer, Japan is now also a leading importer of fish. The country's command is manifested more in terms of its dominance of markets and in Japanese investments in a large number of joint ventures, rather than in terms of fishing capacity in distant waters.

Although meat consumption in Japan is rising, the Japanese are essentially more fond of fish. With a consumption of 72 kg per person per year, they have a decided preference for higher-priced species like prawns, tuna and salmon. Japan's catches of such fish have declined to 7.36 million tonnes in 1994. Yet, incomes continue to rise. This has fuelled imports of marine produce. In 1995, nearly 3.5 million tonnes were shipped into Japan.

Japan's fishing industry has been plagued by problems of labour. This, in turn, has pushed up the average age of the Japanese fisherman. In 1992, 80 per cent of coastal fishermen were over 40, and 34.6 per cent over 60 (see *Fishing News International*, October 1993 and December 1993, and *Supply and Demand of Fish and Fisheries Products in Japan*, Guylaine Bourguignon, IFEP, Paris, July 1992). Today, Japanese tuna fishing companies recruit their crews from the Pacific islands.

Although the size of their catches has remained stable, the incomes of coastal fishermen have not kept pace with incomes in the industrial sector. Income from fishing therefore has to be supplemented by income from other sources.

All sectors of the Japanese fishing industry – industrial and small-scale – are affected by similar problems. Their fishing zones are overexploited and contaminated by pollutants. One reason for this is the creation of 'Exclusive Economic Zones' (EEZs). This development has driven the Japanese away from their traditional distant-water fisheries, particularly from those around the United States. Obliged to fish in their own EEZ and adjacent areas, the Japanese have overexploited their fish stocks. Coastal fishing and aquaculture have survived better, because traditional management of coastal waters by co-operatives has helped protect stocks. However, due to pollution and the dearth of cultivable area, aquaculture alone cannot solve Japan's crisis – and aquaculture can itself cause significant pollution.

Canada

Before 1880

British Columbia

Traps and weirs

After 1880

British Columbia

Purse seines,
gill-nets, trolling

Canada's west-coast fishery

Although salmon fishing in British Columbia provided a major food source long before European settlers arrived, today's multispecies fishery has a relatively short history, dating back some 100 years.

Using a variety of techniques to catch numerous species, the industry has experienced many problems over the last decade or so. More recently, the greatest difficulties facing fisheries are caused by government restructuring programmes. Designed to cut the fleet in half, the Mifflin plan (named after the Canadian Fisheries Minister) will make resource management easier for the government, but will provide a severe blow to coastal communities totally reliant on fishing. The Mifflin plan is reported to have caused the loss of some 7800 jobs.

Historically the entire culture and economy of the native peoples in British Columbia depended on salmon. The resource was managed using complex systems of fishing rights based on family groups, under the leadership of the aboriginal societies. A recent estimate put annual salmon harvests on the Frazer river under this regime, for several millennia prior to the arrival of the Europeans, in excess of 6 million salmon. Since the establishment of a commercial canning industry in the late 1880s, however, salmon stocks have suffered a major decline.

The aboriginal fishery selectively harvested fish with traps and weirs near the spawning grounds to meet immediate needs. However, the modern fishery targets salmon in coastal waters before they enter the rivers, mainly with purse seines and gill-nets and by trolling.

Declining fish stocks and increased catching capacity have prompted management measures which restrict fishing time. Ironically, government policies designed to restrict catching capacity and stop resource depletion have actually increased fishing capacity. Fishers have responded by modernizing their vessels to maintain their share of a declining resource base.

British Columbia also has significant fisheries for spring row-herring, halibut and groundfish (cod-like fish). Herring are caught by purse seine or gill-net, primarily for a Japanese market. Halibut are caught on long-lines for a North American fresh fish market. There is a trawl fishery for groundfish, and a trap fishery for crab. Over the last 10–15 years, many boats have left the salmon industry and have entered the trawl fishery. This has resulted in significant increases in fishing pressure and precipitated new management measures based on strict trip and season quotas, regulated by on-board observers.

These many problems are hastening the demise of a fishery which has provided a way of life for several millennia, but which is now struggling to survive.

Fishing in the USA

Trend in commercial landings, 1986 - 95 Alaska pollack, other Pacific trawl fish

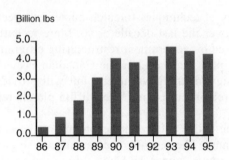

Billion lbs

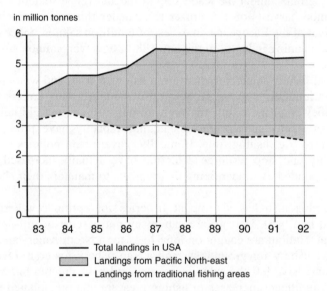

in million tonnes

—— Total landings in USA

▨ Landings from Pacific North-east

- - - - Landings from traditional fishing areas

Trend in commercial landings, 1986 - 95 North Atlantic trawl fish

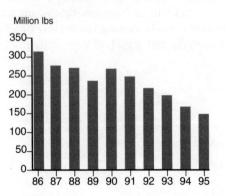

Million lbs

Opportunities from the sea

The USA has by far the largest Exclusive Economic Zone (EEZ), which in 1992 represented 10 per cent of the total area claimed by 122 coastal nations at that time. Over the 1970s and 1980s, when global fish catches increased by roughly one third, fish catches in the USA doubled.

After Japan, the USA is the second largest seafood importer, with food fish imports valued at US$6.8 billion in 1995. Shrimp constituted about 40 per cent of this, being supplied mainly from Equador and Thailand. Thanks to UNCLOS, the USA is now also a major seafood exporter, with seafood exports making a significant contribution to the US economy. In 1995, a year when the commercial marine fishing industry contributed $19.7 million (in value added) to the US gross national product, US fish exports totalled $3.3 billion.

One species dominates fish exports from the USA: Alaska pollack. With landings of 1.3 million tonnes in 1995, Alaska pollack was the most important species in quantity and fourth in value – accounting for 29 per cent of commercial fishery landings in the USA.

Until the early 1980s, fleets from Japan and the former Soviet Union took most of the Alaska pollack catch. These fleets have now been replaced by US fishing fleets. The Northeast Pacific has become the USA's most important fishery zone. In 1970 Alaska accounted for 14 per cent of the US catch; in 1995 it totalled some 2.4 million tonnes, accounting for around 55 per cent of the total US fish catch.

Despite the potential to continue to reap large benefits from their fisheries in the future, many previously rich fisheries of the USA are now threatened by overfishing. For example, on the Grand Banks in New England, overfishing has caused the demise of an industry which provided the mainstay for communities on the North Atlantic coast for centuries. As far back as 1675, some 665 vessels caught between 35 and 40 thousand tonnes of fish. At the end of the 1960s, peak annual catches of around one million tonnes were made. In 1995 the entire fish catch from the New England fishery was roughly one quarter of this – some 270 000 tonnes.

The landings of several high-value species (e.g. cod, haddock and yellow-tail flounder) are now at or close to all-time low values. In some areas, overfishing has resulted in a change of the species composition, from one dominated by high-value cod-like fish, to one dominated by lower-value species. The Northeast Multispecies Fishery Management Plan restricts the gear types that can be used, and enforces seasonal quotas. The Massachusetts Offshore Groundfish Task Force (1990) estimated that if the groundfish stocks were restored, fisheries production could be increased by $350 million annually, and 14 000 jobs could be recovered. (See *The State of the World Fisheries and Aquaculture*, FAO, 1997; *Marine Fisheries and the Law of the Sea: A decade of change*, FAO, 1993; *Fisheries of the United States, 1995*, US Department of Commerce.)

Oyster landings in Maryland

640 000 T

1840 - 90

60 000 T

Around 1900

14 500 T

After 1986

overfishing - habitat destruction by gears -
industrial and municipal wastes - sedimentation - diseases

decline of oyster landings

reduction of cleansing capacity of
oyster population

1986 - Oyster Roundtable

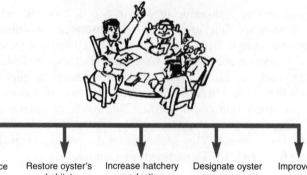

Monitor and reduce
the disease

Restore oyster's
habitat

Increase hatchery
production

Designate oyster
recovery areas

Improve water
quality

Threats from the land

Chesapeake Bay, one of the richest inshore fisheries in the USA, has suffered considerable declines in productivity from overfishing as well as from pollution from mining, agriculture, industry and urban development. Nine major rivers, draining some 64 000 square miles, empty into the Bay, the main stem of which is about 200 miles long and varies in width from 3 to 30 miles. It is the largest and most productive estuary in North America.

Oysters play a key role in cleansing the water by filtering out many harmful bacteria and noxious substances, and archaeological remains and historical records show that the oyster fishery has been of considerable importance since the Chesapeake was formed some 3000 years ago.

Habitat destruction, caused by the use of certain types of fishing gear, and overfishing led to dramatic declines in oyster landings at the end of the nineteenth century. The use of dredges in particular has been cited as the cause of the destruction of the oyster beds, and the principal cause of overfishing. Between 1840 and 1890 annual landings in Maryland averaged 600 000 tonnes. By the early 1900s landings had declined to 80 000 tonnes, and since 1986 annual landings have remained under 15 000 tonnes. In the entire Chesapeake Bay, oyster landings dropped from 14 500 tonnes in 1959 to under 500 tonnes in 1990. In 1993 the Bay-wide oyster catch plummeted an estimated 270 tonnes (600 000 lbs).

In more recent years population pressure and industrial development are cited as causes of deteriorating water quality and the outbreak of disease which have added to the devastation of oyster populations. Toxic chemical waste from mining, industry and agriculture, including heavy metals, PCBs and pesticides, have accumulated in Bay sediments. The release of industrial and municipal waste into the Bay has increased. Increasing levels of sedimentation resulting from run-off into the Bay has caused further degradation of the aquatic environment. Oysters are particularly sensitive to such pollution and habitat degradation.

Due to the demise of the oyster, the self-cleaning capacity of the environment has also been greatly impaired. When the Europeans first came to the USA, oysters in the Chesapeake Bay could filter the volume of water in the Bay in two weeks. Now, because so few remain, they take more than a year (see *Net Loss: Fish, jobs and the marine environment*, 1994, World Watch Paper 120).

In 1989 the Chesapeake Bay Program established an oyster management plan with the goal of conserving oyster stocks while maintaining a viable fishery. Efforts to date have included research into the demise of the oyster and the restoration of the environment. A recent initiative in Maryland has brought together 40 representatives including fishworkers, academics, state officials, environmentalists, and aquaculturists in an 'Oyster Roundtable'. They have produced an action plan with several specific recommendations, which recognizes the ecological importance of the oyster as well as its commercial value.

China ranks among leading fish producers

Growth of Chinese fish production

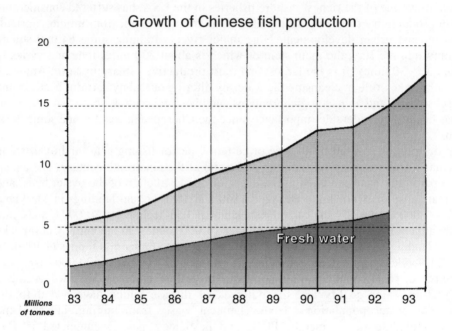

Millions
of tonnes

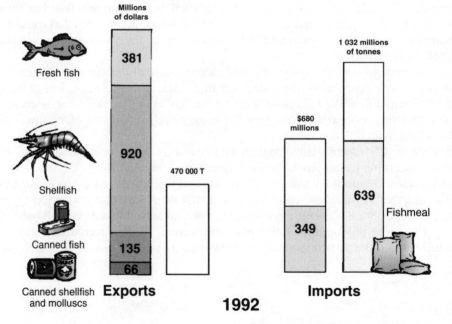

Millions
of dollars

Fresh fish   **381**

Shellfish   **920**

470 000 T

Canned fish   **135**

Canned shellfish
and molluscs   **66**

Exports

1 032 millions
of tonnes

$680
millions

639   Fishmeal

349

Imports

1992

Source : *Fishing News International*, December 1994.

© A Le Sann – CRISLA, 1995

China emerges as a fishing power

In 1980, the total catch of fish in China was 4.5 million tonnes. By 1994, it was estimated to have touched 20.7 million tonnes, 18 per cent more than the previous year's figure of 17.5 million tonnes. Today, China accounts for a total catch close to 20 per cent of the world's fish production.

How did such a dramatic rise occur? The answer in one word – aquaculture. The industrial development of aquaculture in coastal waters or inland lakes was largely responsible for the growth in Chinese fish production – accounting for more than half the total quantity fished. Chinese freshwater fisheries can now artificially reproduce carp, without having to capture wild larvae. The liberalization of the economy has also played a part in the development of fisheries. So has the abandonment of agricultural collectives. This favoured the development of fish farms to meet growing demand. Today, four million hectares (ten million acres) are used to raise fish. Marine aquaculture is also on the increase in response to demand for molluscs, algae and, above all, prawns. This required imports of vast amounts of fishmeal, totalling 639 000 tonnes in 1992.

China's freshwater fishing, as well as coastal aquaculture units, are increasingly threatened by pollution. Both inshore and deep-sea fish stocks are dwindling. This fact, coupled with technological backwardness, has forced China into fishing far away in African offshore waters and in the North Pacific. More than 35 joint ventures have been set up to fish the waters of 50 countries to supply the Chinese markets, as well as export demand. In 1993, there were nearly 6000 joint ventures in the fishing and aquaculture sectors (see *Fishing News International*, December 1994, p. 48).

In the long term, the viability of this kind of development is suspect. For one thing, shrimp aquaculture is threatened by increasing pollution. For another, there are recurring problems of access to certain Russian fishing zones. Moreover, nationally owned ocean-going trawlers have to face problems of management and profitability (see *Samudra*, Nos. 10–11, December 1994 and *Atlas des pêches et cultures maritimes*, Jean Chaussade and Jean-Pierre Corlay, Le Marin, 1990). There are also ongoing tensions, notably with Vietnam, over the delimitation of Exclusive Economic Zones (EEZs).

The boom in fish production in China may continue to be insufficient to supply its domestic market. Yet, the opportunities for developing a well-organized inland aquaculture have been clearly demonstrated in China.

The South now produces more than the North

Marine fish catches

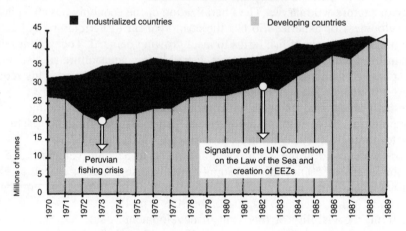

- ■ Industrialized countries
- ▨ Developing countries

Millions of tonnes

Peruvian fishing crisis

Signature of the UN Convention on the Law of the Sea and creation of EEZs

Total marine and freshwater catches

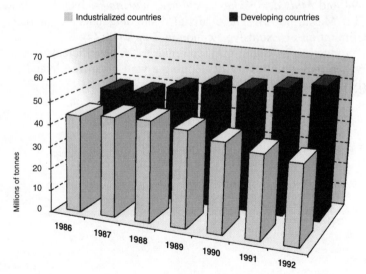

- ▨ Industrialized countries
- ■ Developing countries

Millions of tonnes

Source : FAO

In the South, fishing is on the increase

The worldwide increase in fishing activity, particularly during the 1980s, has largely sprung from Southern countries. Today, 11 of them figure among the 22 leading fish producing countries of the world. Since 1989, production in the South has tended to outstrip that of developed countries, where catch figures have remained steady or have even fallen. The principal fishing powers of the South (Chile, Peru and China) continue to develop, while the giants of the North either waver, like Japan, or collapse, like Russia.

Worldwide, the production figures for both marine and inland fishing show a rise in production in Southern countries, and a collapse of fish catches in the North. The growth in the catch figures for the South needs to be qualified, however, since neither South Korea nor Taiwan can be included among the poorer countries.

The South's growth results from various developments. The introduction of EEZs shifted the attention of many countries to the value of hitherto underexploited resources. Most of these countries get the bulk of their catches in their own EEZs. The few exceptions are South Korea, Taiwan and, more recently, China, which has deployed its fleet around Africa and in the Pacific.

The other factor is the rise of industrial fishing, even though Southern fisheries are largely dominated by the artisanal sector using dug-outs or other small craft. In several countries, often through joint ventures, industrial fishing fleets have been developed for fishmeal production, as is spectacularly the case in South America, particularly in Chile.

Also significant is the growth of freshwater catches. These have more than doubled in Asia during the 1980s, a growth of 115 per cent. Such fisheries are of particular importance for some landlocked countries with lakes or rivers, like Uganda, Egypt, Chad and Tanzania, or for those with abundant water supplies, like India, China, the Philippines and Vietnam.

Three aquaculture systems

Restocking and sea ranching	Rural aquaculture (extensive production)	Intensive production
Controlled reproduction ▼ Culture of juvenile fish ▼ Restocking the wild ▼ Growth in the wild ▼ Capture in the wild	Hatcheries, or collection of larvae and small fry in the wild Culture in controlled or natural environments Reliance on natural food production Limited use of supplemented feeds	Hatchery - collection in natural environment ↓ Culture in controlled environments ↓ Intensive production Intensive use of supplementary feeds

▨ Controlled environment

Source : Ph. Favrelière

© A Le Sann – CRISLA, 1995

Aquaculture gains in stature

Aquaculture is the practice of rearing aquatic plants and animals in a modified environment. It ranges from 'intensive aquaculture', which involves a high degree of control over the production process and with a high level of inputs (feed, fertilizer and management) to 'extensive aquaculture', which may involve little more than manipulating natural production, for example by controlling which fish are stocked, and uses few inputs.

Aquaculture is the farming of aquatic organisms. Farming implies some form of human intervention in the rearing process in order to enhance production. There are, however, many grey areas between aquaculture and fisheries, which may include 'culture-based fisheries', 'ranching' and 'stock enhancement'. Aquaculture may also include other activities associated with replenishing dwindling fish stocks, as well as fishing aided by artificial reefs or brush-parks.

According to the degree of control exerted and inputs made, aquaculture may be classified under three main headings:

- *Extensive* aquaculture transforms an aquatic ecosystem's primary productivity (organic matter produced by photosynthesis) into products for consumption by humans. It generally requires few external inputs (e.g. supplementary feeding, fertilizer, etc.).
- *Semi-intensive* aquaculture builds on extensive systems and may require supplementary feeding and other inputs. Semi-intensive aquaculture includes traditional Asian 'polyculture' systems, where several species are stocked which occupy complementary ecological niches. This makes optimum use of both space and food resources. It may also include integrated aquaculture, where aquaculture is combined with agriculture; for example, combining fish and rice cultivation (as in South-east Asia), or the combined culturing of shellfish and seaweed.
- *Intensive* aquaculture involves much higher stocking rates, and the use of supplementary feeds (often using fishmeal in the form of protein-rich granules) to meet all the needs of the species being raised. On average, 3 kg of feed are needed to produce 1 kg of fish (see *Sea Food International*, May 1995, p. 7). More and more species, including tuna and cod, are being raised in this way.

Aquaculture may also involve restocking the natural environment, as is the case in sport fisheries and in some salmon fisheries. The latter is often called 'ranching', and may entail hatchery production and the raising of juvenile fish before they are eventually released into the wild. Juvenile fish are thus protected during the most vulnerable stages of their development.

In 1993, global aquaculture (including seaweed culture) accounted for 19 million tonnes or nearly 20 per cent of all fish catches. This was an increase of 70 per cent over the 1984 figure. Today, many people argue that aquaculture offers the only alternative means to maintain or increase fish supplies in the face of decreasing fish catches (see *Fishing News International*, April 1995).

The prawn farming boom

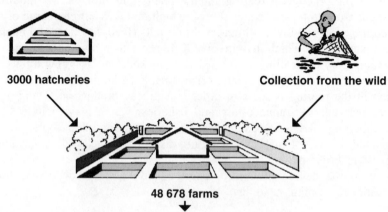

3000 hatcheries

Collection from the wild

48 678 farms

1 000 000 ha tanks or ponds producing 720kg / ha

1991 - Production from prawn aquaculture

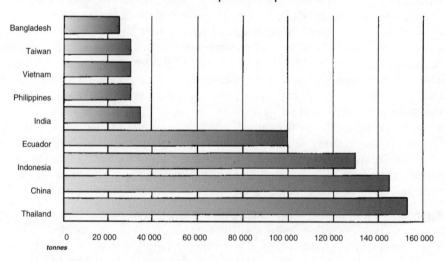

Bangladesh
Taiwan
Vietnam
Philippines
India
Ecuador
Indonesia
China
Thailand

0   20 000   40 000   60 000   80 000   100 000   120 000   140 000   160 000

tonnes

733 000 tonnes
from aquaculture

1 867 000 tonnes
caught from the wild

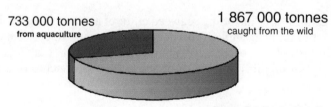

Source: Fish Farming International December 1992

© A Le Sann – CRISLA, 1995

Intensive aquaculture becomes the modern-day gold rush

Traditionally, the aim of aquaculture was to make the best of agricultural by-products, exploiting the natural potential of the environment. Subsequently, from the 1960s onwards, a new objective emerged: to satisfy the rapidly burgeoning demand for fish in Northern countries. As a result, salmon and shrimp culture took off during the 1980s. Salmon production rose from 33 951 tonnes in 1984 to 293 658 tonnes in 1991, while shrimp culture touched 721 000 tonnes in 1991, up from a mere 50 000 tonnes in 1980.

Aquaculture has been developed along intensive lines, mostly by industrial and other commercial concerns. These new production systems require substantial investment and skilled management. Their growth and expansion have been led by the large agribusinesses (namely, feed and equipment manufacturers and suppliers of fingerlings). The aim of these companies was immediate profit, rather than a development policy designed to reduce the global shortfall in fish production. Fish species were favoured which had a high value and demand in international markets, such as salmon, trout, prawns, bass, bream and turbot.

Farmed shrimps were first imported into France in 1987. By 1992, they made up more than half of the country's tropical prawn imports, mainly from Thailand, Ecuador, Indonesia and China. In Norway, farmed salmon production rose dramatically from 4000 tonnes in 1979 to 200 000 tonnes in 1994, causing prices to fall. Consequently, the current potential of the hatcheries – 300 000 tonnes – cannot be fully exploited (see *Seafood International*, September 1994, pp. 22–35). In China, deterioration of the environment and the resultant disease caused prawn culture production to fall from 140 000 tonnes in 1991 to 50 000 tonnes in 1992.

Importantly, traditional aquaculture fully exploits not only the potential of the environment but also agricultural by-products. In contrast, modern aquaculture depends upon supplementary feeds, like intensive pig and poultry rearing systems. Most of the species raised are carnivores, which have to be fed food rich in animal protein, such as fishmeal. Ultimately, aquaculture seems merely to convert food from one form into another, but adding considerable economic value to it in the process. In essence, as the experiences of various countries show, these intensive models of aquaculture have proved to be fragile, economically as well as ecologically.

Growth of imports in the North

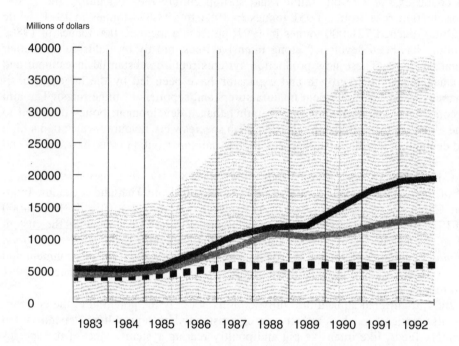

Millions of dollars

EU

Japan

United States

Total for developed countries

Source : FAO

The North imports more

In countries of the North, fish production has been dwindling for several years – from 46 million tonnes in 1988 to 36.3 million tonnes in 1992. It now accounts for no more than 39.3 per cent of global production. This fall in production is due to the overexploitation of fish stocks and the loss of fishing areas after the establishment of Exclusive Economic Zones (EEZs).

Consumption, however, is steadily rising in Northern countries, which are importing ever-greater quantities of fish. The value of their imports rose from $14.5 billion in 1983 to $38.7 billion in 1992, accounting for 85 per cent of world imports.

The imports comprise mainly species with high commercial value, such as prawns and tuna, in addition to fishmeal and fish oil. The principal importers are Japan, the United States, France, Spain, Italy, Germany and the United Kingdom. The European Union (EU) leads, with annual imports worth $16.6 billion, compared with $12.8 billion for Japan. The EU, which produces about six million tonnes per year, imports three million tonnes, of which a quarter originates in Southern countries such as Thailand, Morocco, Senegal and Argentina (see Courier ACP-CEE, No 129, September–October 1991, pp. 37–39). Within the EU, France imports more than Spain, in terms of value.

Initially, these imports were intended to supplement national production. However, the diversity of the fish species imported tends to turn them into a source of competition. Certain species fight for shelf space in the markets with catches from the North, such as hake, sea-bream and tuna. They therefore push down prices.

Growth of exports from the South

Value of world seafood exports

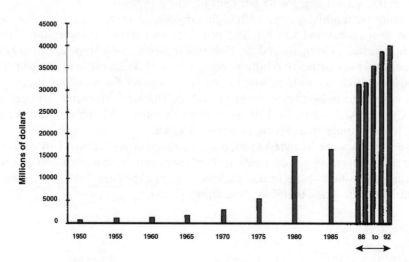

Share of developing and industrialized countries in world exports

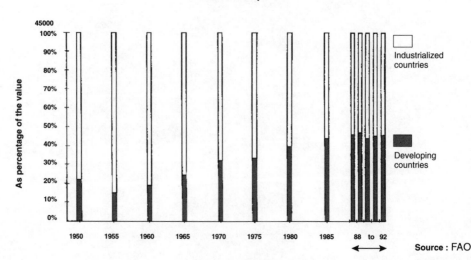

Source : FAO

The South exports more

As fishing activities expand in the South, they are becoming increasingly caught up in global market systems. The South's contribution to the international fish trade is constantly increasing. Between 1981 and 1991, the value of exports from Southern countries rose by 163 per cent to reach $17.4 billion or 45.3 per cent of the value of exports worldwide.

Taking into account the South's modest level of imports (14 per cent of the world total), the balance of trade for marine produce from Southern countries yields a surplus of over $11 billion, double that earned by coffee, a traditional export commodity. However, the statistics provided by the FAO classify South Korea and Taiwan as developing countries, whereas their current fishing capacities would justify their inclusion among the developed countries.

This substantial growth in exports has made the seafood market among the most dynamic and globalized. In 1990, more than 36 per cent of the value of world production of seafood was exported. Although Southern countries concentrate on products with a high market value, like shrimps, tuna and crayfish, they also sell lower-priced products such as fishmeal or fish oil, used as animal feed for pigs, poultry and fish. Most of the farms that use this feed are in the North; those in the South which use such feed are usually oriented towards export – of shrimps, for example.

The leading exporters are the Asian countries of Thailand, South Korea, Indonesia and China and, in South America, Chile, Ecuador and Peru. In 1993, according to the FAO's 1995 edition of *The State of World Fisheries and Aquaculture*, Thailand became the world's top exporter. Some African countries, including Morocco, Senegal, Mauritania, the Ivory Coast and South Africa, have rapidly developed their exports. For many Southern countries, such as Peru, Chile, Senegal, Bangladesh and Mauritania, seafood exports have become a primary source of hard currency. This development may well please advocates of economic liberalization but, overall, for the exporting countries themselves, it has had a negative impact on the environment and on food security. The net effect of this global trade is a transfer of protein from the South to the North.

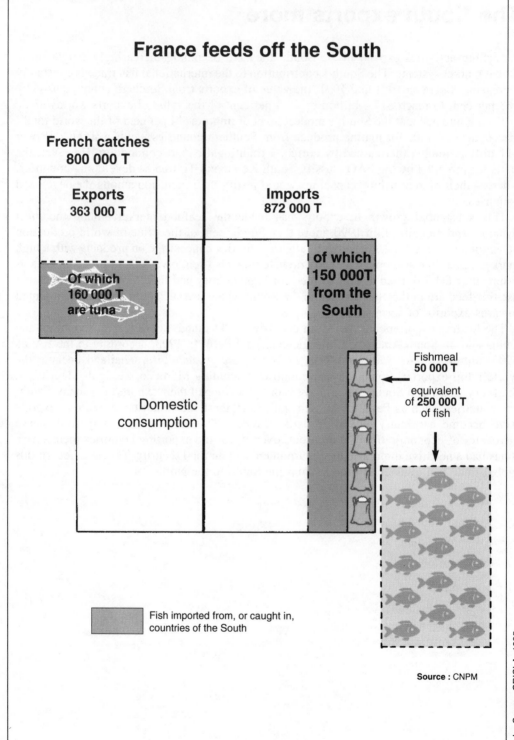

France feeds off the South

**French catches
800 000 T**

**Exports
363 000 T**

**Imports
872 000 T**

Of which
160 000 T
are tuna

**of which
150 000T
from the
South**

Fishmeal
50 000 T

equivalent
of **250 000 T**
of fish

Domestic
consumption

Fish imported from, or caught in,
countries of the South

Source : CNPM

© A Le Sann – CRISLA, 1995

France feeds off the South

For a number of years, fish consumption in France has been increasing steadily. At the same time, domestic production has dropped too low to meet demand. As a result, there has been a spectacular increase in imports, from 500 000 tonnes in 1980 to 872 000 tonnes in 1992. Since 1989, annual exports have been more than 300 000 tonnes. Although they reached 363 000 tonnes in 1992, the demand–supply gap for the year was still over 500 000 tonnes. The cost of this deficit is high. It represents France's largest deficit in the agrifood market. In value, it corresponds to the surpluses generated by dairy exports.

Of the 1.2 million tonnes of fish products consumed each year, two out of every three fish bought in France originate overseas. The South is the main supplier, particularly if the fresh fish equivalent of fishmeal is also taken into account. (Official statistics include a range of products – fresh fish, frozen and tinned fish as well as fishmeal.) In 1992 alone, more than 50 000 tonnes of fishmeal were imported from the South, the equivalent of 250 000 tonnes of fresh fish.

Similarly, it should be noted that a major part of the total fish imports consists of processed products derived from a larger quantity of fresh fish caught in the country of origin. Calculated thus, French imports amount to an equivalent of 1 200 000 tonnes of fresh fish, much of which originates in the South.

Next to salmon, in terms of value as well as quantity, prawns and tuna feature as major imports, mostly from the South. If fishmeal (or, more correctly, its fresh fish equivalent) is also considered, the South can be said to produce around 400 000 tonnes of France's total fish consumption. For every three fish consumed in France, one is fished in European waters by French boats, another comes from a country in the South, while the third is imported from Europe or North America. The South figures prominently in French exports as well. Around 40 per cent consist of frozen tuna fished by French boats off West African coasts or in the Indian Ocean (see *Le commerce extérieur des produits de la mer*, CNPM, 1992).

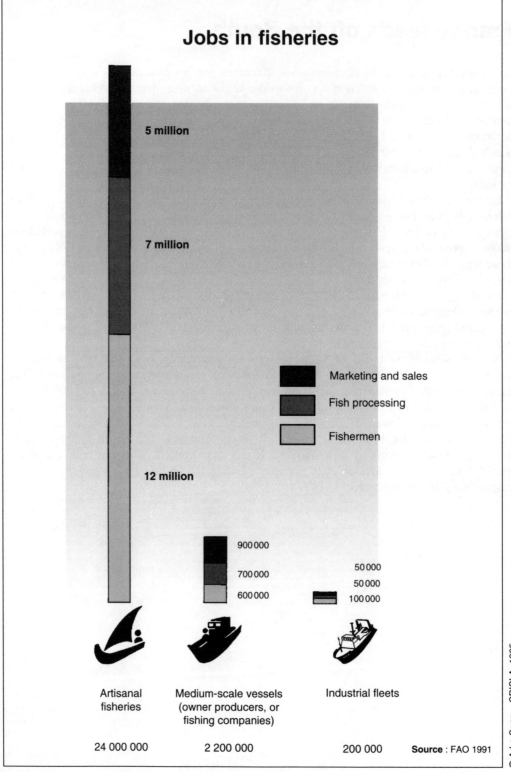

Jobs in fisheries

5 million

7 million

Marketing and sales

Fish processing

Fishermen

12 million

900 000

700 000

600 000

50 000

50 000

100 000

Artisanal fisheries	Medium-scale vessels (owner producers, or fishing companies)	Industrial fleets
24 000 000	2 200 000	200 000

Source : FAO 1991

© A Le Sann – CRISLA, 1995

Artisanal fishing creates jobs

Around the world, between 12 and 13 million registered fishermen are directly involved in the business of catching fish. To this can be added all the jobs that result from associated activities: every industrial or artisanal fishing port generates economic activities such as boatbuilding, engine maintenance, ice production, and manufacture of fishing gear.

In fisheries, the processing, transportation and, particularly, distribution sectors produce a multitude of jobs, since both fresh and processed fish need careful handling and packaging, as well as efficient methods of transport.

The artisanal fisheries sector is labour intensive. It provides those with little or no capital the scope to earn a living through traditional types of processing (drying or smoking) or through selling small quantities of fish in local markets. The FAO estimates that each fisherman's job creates two other jobs in processing or distribution. Other sources estimate that a single fishing job at sea creates as many as five jobs in ancillary professions.

In several parts of the world, entire communities live by fishing; some regional or national economies depend almost entirely on the sea and on the state of fish stocks and markets. Such communities often have specific cultural characteristics which must be taken into account when planning development programmes. In the event of a crisis, the survival of the fishery can depend as much on the community's overall capacity to react as on the state of fish stocks. Thus, in France, while some areas have seen their entire fishing industry disappear, other neighbouring fishing communities have managed to survive, thanks to their resourcefulness.

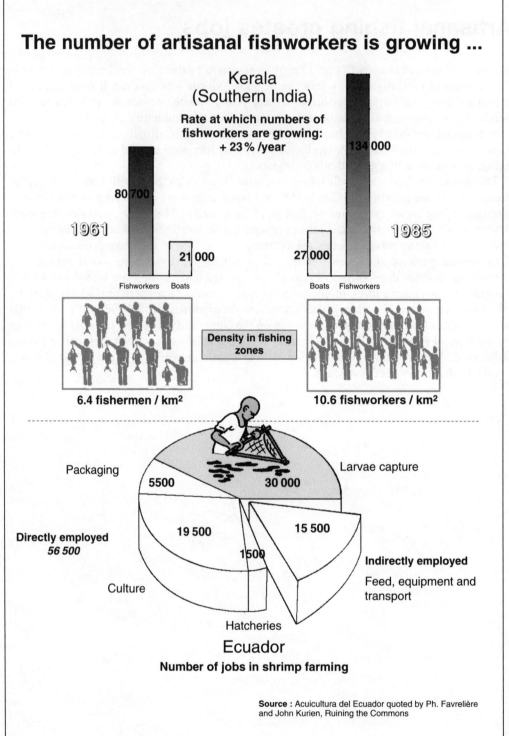

The number of artisanal fishworkers is growing ...

Kerala
(Southern India)

**Rate at which numbers of
fishworkers are growing:
+ 23 % /year**

1961

80 700

21 000

Fishworkers   Boats

134 000

1985

27 000

Boats   Fishworkers

**Density in fishing
zones**

6.4 fishermen / km²

10.6 fishworkers / km²

Packaging

Larvae capture

5500

30 000

19 500

15 500

**Directly employed
*56 500***

1500

Indirectly employed

Feed, equipment and
transport

Culture

Hatcheries

Ecuador
Number of jobs in shrimp farming

Source : Acuicultura del Ecuador quoted by Ph. Favrelière
and John Kurien, Ruining the Commons

© A Le Sann – CRISLA, 1995

Artisanal fishworkers are growing in number

According to the FAO, worldwide there are 13 million registered fishermen. This figure would, of course, be much greater if the large numbers of unregistered fishermen were included. Not all fishermen are full time: some of them operate seasonally, supplementing other sources of income. The International Collective in Support of Fishworkers (ICSF), an international NGO, prefers to use the term 'fishworker', rather than 'fisherman', as the former more appropriately covers the gamut of jobs related to fishing, and also includes women involved in processing, selling fish and all the other closely allied activities typical of fishing communities.

In Southern countries, thousands of women and children participate in activities such as harvesting algae and gathering juvenile fish, larvae and shellfish. In developed countries, too, thousands make their living by gathering shellfish in the inter-tidal zone, without being officially registered as fishermen. France, for example, has around 20 000 registered fishermen, with an unknown number of people who engage in part-time or sport fishing.

In many countries, as much in the North as in the South, economic crisis has forced many poorer people to search for alternative livelihoods and/or to eke out a living in the coastal areas. In Veys Bay in Normandy, France, over a few years, the number of (mostly unemployed) people gathering cockles along the shore, without the use of boats, rose from 100 to 400. However, the creation of a producers' organization has enabled 120 people to register as fishworkers, all paying tax and social security contributions. On the island of Chiloe in Chile, 10 000 people were harvesting algae in 1984, but today there are no more than 400 (see *Tout pour la farine de poisson*, Philippe Favrelière, Lettre de Solagral, 1989). Senegal's beaches attract numerous people fleeing the drought and poverty of their rural origins.

Most of the world's fishworkers are artisanal and often very poor. They are often as numerous inland as along the coast. In Columbia, for example, of 110 000 fishworkers 80 000 work on lakes and rivers.

The role of women in Japan

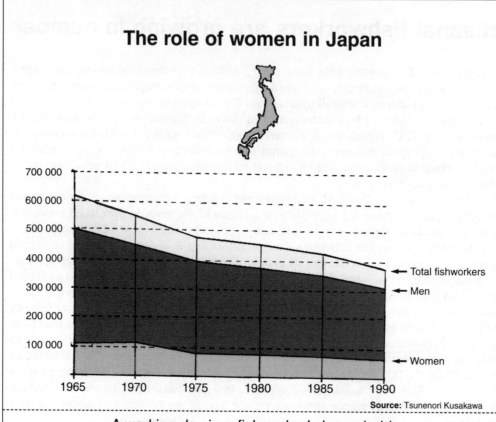

Source: Tsunenori Kusakawa

A working day in a fishworker's household

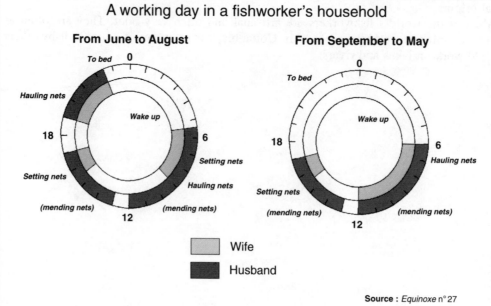

Source : *Equinoxe* n° 27

© A Le Sann – CRISLA, 1995

The role of women is ignored

The fishing industry, especially the catching side, is generally considered to be a man's world, even though women may play an important role. Women participate in large numbers to collect prawn larvae and to fish for fingerlings to stock aquaculture ponds. They also harvest algae and shellfish. In oyster farming in France, the women often accompany their husbands to the oyster beds.

In Southern countries, women sometimes participate in subsistence fishing. Pre-catch activities increasingly involve women, who prepare lines and make nets. In the state of Bengal in India, for example, there are several thousand women net-makers. They are also often key players at the first point of sale, and make an important contribution to the local economy, sustaining decentralized systems for processing and marketing fish. Such a role is also of crucial importance to household income and food security, and in the wider distribution of fish in the local community.

In Northern countries such as Canada, Norway and Japan, the crises in the industry often force women in the family to replace existing crew members, particularly if her boat-owner husband (or other family member) is no longer able to pay for crew wages.

It is in the post-harvest stages of fishing that the role of women is most prominent. Both in the North and in the South, they are the ones who process and market the fish, in the artisanal as well as in the industrial sector. In Western Africa and in Asia, 70–80 per cent of marine produce is marketed by women (see *Conserver et transformer le poisson*, CTA-GRET, 1993, p. 290).

In the industrial sector, working conditions are often tough, since much of the work has to be done in cold and damp conditions with a minimum of social security (see *La situation des femmes chez les gens de mer*, CRISLA, 1994). In India, more than 25 000 young girls from the State of Kerala work far from home in shrimp factories for several months of the year. In the artisanal sector, women rarely benefit from any financial aid and have to make do with the most rudimentary processing and marketing infrastructure.

It is noteworthy that women are sometimes able to control fishing activities through their ability to finance fishing operations. In many instances it is the work undertaken by women that underwrites or provides the risk fund necessary to sustain fishing activities. In general, though, they are largely ignored by the State and other formal organizations.

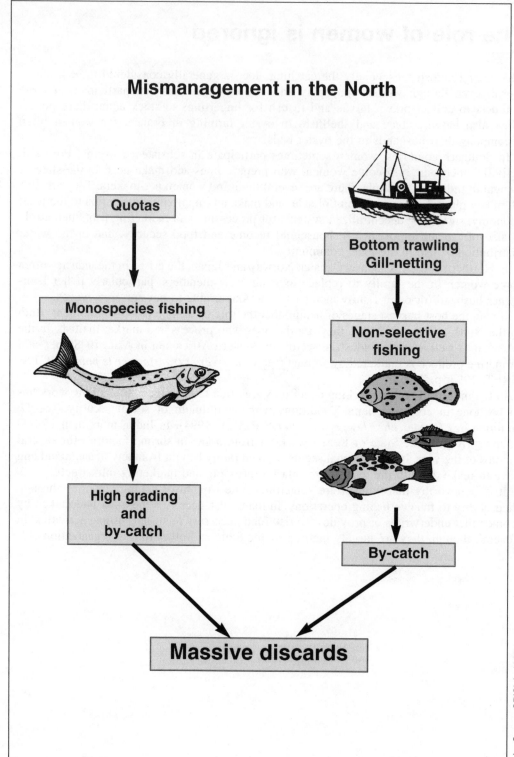

Mismanagement in the North

Quotas

Monospecies fishing

High grading and by-catch

Bottom trawling Gill-netting

Non-selective fishing

By-catch

Massive discards

Quotas and fisheries mismanagement in the North

'By-catch', 'high grading' and 'discards' describe some of the most wasteful and damaging practices in modern commercial fisheries. They are the direct result of fisheries management systems based on quotas. An FAO-commissioned global assessment of fisheries by-catch and discards estimates that some 27 million tonnes, or over 30 per cent of fish are discarded (i.e. dumped, usually after they are dead) annually (*A Global Assessment of Fisheries Bycatch and Discards*, Alverson, D., et al. FAO Technical Paper 339, 1994).

- *By-catch* is the incidental or unintentional part of the catch. Sometimes valuable, but often not, in many cases it is dumped back into the sea as discards.
- *High grading* processes the catch to keep fish of the highest quality and economic value, while discarding fish of lower value and quality (bruised, spoiled, etc.). High grading maximizes the catch rate, but minimizes what is retained to within quota limits. It maximizes the economic return at the expense of the environment and future generations of fish stocks and fishworkers.
- *Discards* are the fish and other biomass dumped back into the sea during the fishing operation – more often than not dead or moribund.

The above-cited 1994 FAO report estimates that the by-catch of fin fish in shrimp trawls alone is between 4.5 and 19 million tonnes (roughly 5–20 per cent of the world's entire sea fish catch). In all demersal (bottom) trawl fisheries by-catch rates are unacceptably high (50–80 per cent of the catch), with unknown damage inflicted on the life-supporting ecosystem. Gill-netters in the North Pacific reportedly catch 200 unintended species – 40 per cent of the total catch weight.

The introduction of quota management has encouraged 'monospecies fishing' (the practice of targeting single species of high commercial value). This results in many non-target species, over-quota fish and small fish being discarded and wasted, or landed and sold as 'black fish' – i.e. illegally on the black market.

As well as having implications for resource depletion and marine biodiversity, discards and by-catch represent a huge potential source of economic wealth and protein-rich food, which is currently wasted.

SECTION 2
KEY ISSUES

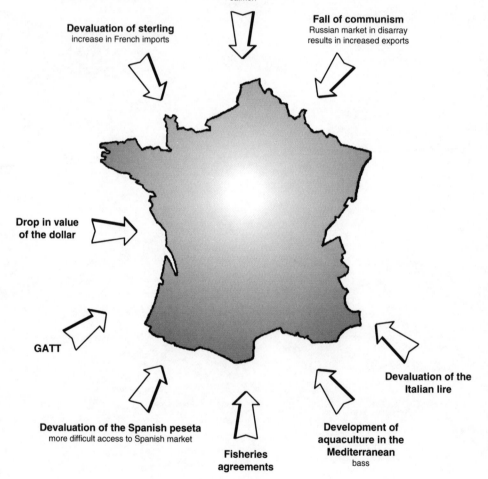

External factors affecting the French fishing crisis
1993 - 94

Norwegian aquaculture
salmon

Devaluation of sterling
increase in French imports

Fall of communism
Russian market in disarray
results in increased exports

**Drop in value
of the dollar**

GATT

Devaluation of the Spanish peseta
more difficult access to Spanish market

**Fisheries
agreements**

**Development of
aquaculture in the
Mediterranean**
bass

**Devaluation of the
Italian lire**

Globalization is spreading

The fishing industry is one of the most highly globalized economic sectors. Today, nearly 40 per cent of total global fish production is traded on the international market. Naturally, all fishworkers are directly or indirectly affected by these transactions.

Some countries have maintained and developed distant-water fishing fleets, but the dominant tendency is towards consolidating trade and market shares. Thus, the Japanese government supports the development of local industrial or artisanal fleets by, for example, providing motors for fishing boats, so as to encourage export advantages for Japan.

Falling transport costs facilitate the relocation of processing industries seeking cheap labour. Product-specific markets are now being invaded by substitutes. European langoustines (Dublin Bay prawn or Nephrops), for example, now have to compete with either captured or cultured tropical shrimps. Similarly, the crab market is increasingly challenged by surimi, a fish paste which is often made by Japanese companies from fish caught in American waters.

The market for fish is also influenced by the global trade in other food products, and by economic policy decisions in other areas. A fall in the price of cereals means lower prices for meat, causing fish to become a luxury food. The collapse of the Soviet Union caused a boom in Russian exports. The devaluation of the CFA franc in West Africa in 1994 encouraged export-oriented activities – as happened in Senegal – while reduced incomes in Africa depressed demand on the domestic market.

Around the same time, in 1993 and 1994, French fishermen violently raised the issue of market control by calling for community preference – a protectionist system which favoured European fish over non-European produce. This ran contrary to the dominant tendency towards market liberalization, as set out in the GATT negotiations.

In 1995, an American company has sold ten automated long-line systems for installation on ten 170–foot Russian trawlers. The operation was financed by the Japanese, and the equipment was installed by a Korean shipyard. The fish caught in the Pacific will be sold to Norway for processing and sale on the European market.

(Source: *Fishing News International*, February 1995)

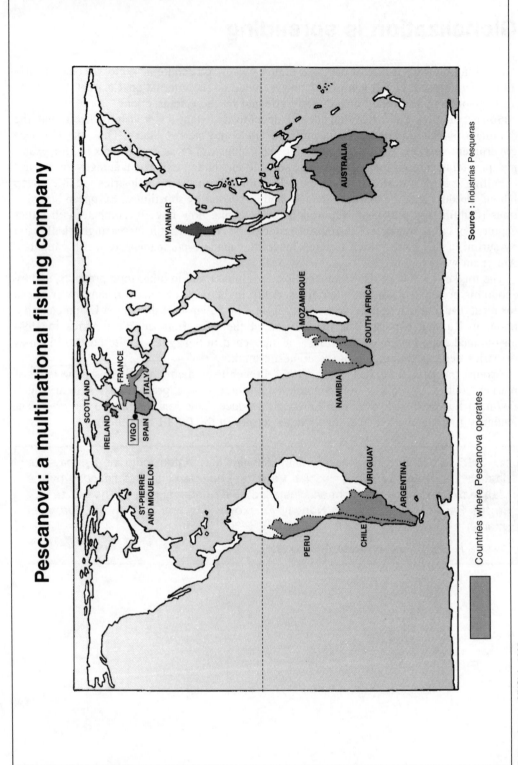

Pescanova: a multinational fishing company

Source : Industrias Pesqueras

Countries where Pescanova operates

ST-PIERRE AND MIQUELON

IRELAND
SCOTLAND
FRANCE
ITALY
VIGO
SPAIN

MYANMAR

AUSTRALIA

MOZAMBIQUE
NAMIBIA
SOUTH AFRICA

PERU
CHILE
URUGUAY
ARGENTINA

Multinationals play a powerful role

In fishing, as in many other industries, production, processing and marketing are increasingly controlled by multinational corporations. For example Unilever, Kraft Foods, and Nestlé all have major stakes in the fishing industry. They control significant proportions of the global fish stocks, dominate global trade, and wield huge influence with governments. Starkist, a large US tuna fishing company, controls a significant part of the global tuna production. Kjell Inge Rokke of Norway control about 10 per cent of the world's white fish production. This company also managed to obtain a sum of grant monies from the Norwegian Government in 1995/96, to build 16 new factory freezer trawlers for Russia, exceeding all the monies granted to the entire Norwegian coastal fishery put together.

The Spanish fishing company Pescanova is one of the five largest in the world, dealing mainly in frozen seafood. It owns half the market share for frozen produce in Spain and, having chosen to concentrate on hake, now handles 20 per cent of the global hake production. The group was set up in the 1960s in Galicia. It embarked on an expansionist marketing strategy of forming joint ventures with countries in the South. A South African company, Imperial Cold Storage, owns 21 per cent of the group's equity, but majority control still resides with the Fernandez de Souza family. Today, Pescanova owns a fleet of more than 140 boats (mostly freezer trawlers), seven factories and 25 000 retail outlets.

The group has considerable influence over the Galician economy, but plays an equally important role in the economies of the Southern countries (e.g. Mozambique and Namibia). Pescanova has preferred to establish local production facilities, rather than to take advantage of international fisheries agreements. This has proved particularly profitable in Namibia, where Pescanova has built a hake filleting factory with a 21 000-tonne capacity: 90 per cent of the total production is exported to Spain.

Pescanova's production is oriented mainly towards markets in the Iberian peninsula, but the company is currently reinforcing its presence in other European countries. Its recent takeover of the Jégo-Quéré group (with substantial subsidy from the French government and from the European Union) is testimony of Pescanova's particular interest in the French market.

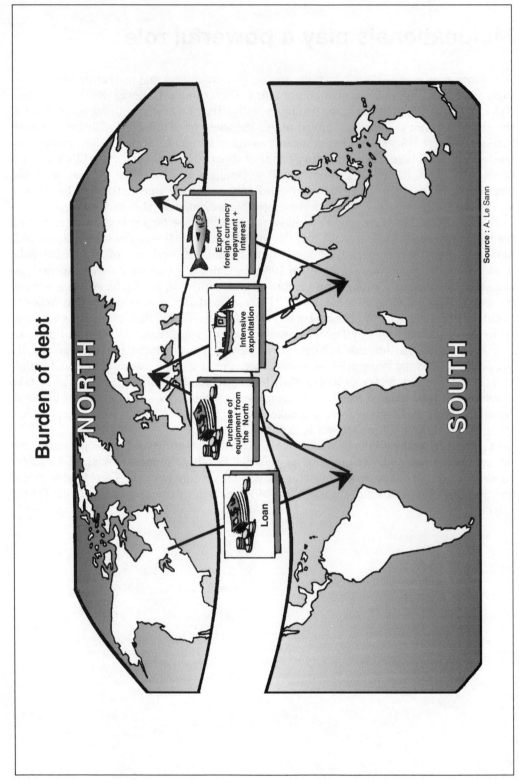

Burden of debt

NORTH

SOUTH

Export – foreign currency repayment + interest

Intensive exploitation

Purchase of equipment from the North

Loan

Source : A. Le Sann

Fishing helps repay Third World debt

In a growing number of Southern countries, exports from fishing and aquaculture earn hard currency that is vitally needed for debt repayment. Traditional leading exporters of fish-meal like Chile and Peru are now being joined by new fishing powers such as Thailand, Indonesia and the Philippines. Senegal's most important export is fish, which earns even more revenue than groundnuts (peanuts), the country's traditional cash crop.

Often, however, this kind of export policy, which gives foreign markets priority over home markets, puts pressure on countries to overexploit their resources, and to deplete their fish stocks, resulting in chronic overfishing. Inevitably, industrial fishing and commercial aquaculture take precedence over artisanal fishing.

In Mauritania, development of industrial fishing has resulted in a complete fiasco. In order for the industry to function, it has to call on expensive Korean experts and to import costly equipment. In some countries the earnings from fish exports do not cover the cost of modernization. Sadly, the reality is that, since almost all the South's production from industrial fishing is exported, it is the developed countries' consumption which is actually being subsidized.

Artisanal fisheries can produce for export as well, at a much lower cost. Being less dependent on costly imported materials and having lower energy requirements, they are much more efficient. In Senegal, half of all marine produce for export comes from artisanal fishing. Industrial fishing, on the other hand, is floundering, despite aid of all kinds. Analysis showed that by the 1980s, the value added in industrial fishing was very low (around 20 per cent) and its contribution to gross domestic product was negligible (about 1 per cent). Industrial fishing units were already working at 30 per cent below their minimum profitability levels. Only with the help of government subsidies could their activities continue. In contrast, in the artisanal sector, the value added was between 50 and 75 per cent of turnover, depending on the type of fishing method used (see *A propos des pêches industrielles au Sénégal*, Catherine Aubertin, Cahiers Sciences Humaines ORSTOM, No. 1, pp. 107–123, 1984).

In October 1994, the Cameroon had some of its debt written off in exchange for a commitment to purchase 50 Spanish shrimp trawlers.

(*Fishing News International*, October 1994)

The cost of over-investment

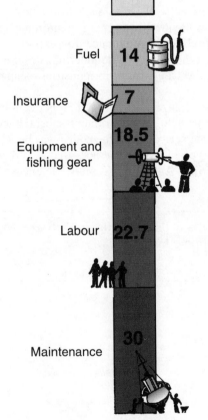

1989 estimates
Source : FAO, 1992

Depreciation and financial charges — 54

Fuel — 14

Insurance — 7

Equipment and fishing gear — 18.5

Labour — 22.7

Maintenance — 30

Overall running cost in billions of dollars

70

Value of world fisheries production

Too much capital invested in global fisheries

Alarmed by the fact that so many oceans are already overfished, the FAO attempted to evaluate the costs of, and the revenues from, fishing. This was a tricky exercise, given the unreliability of statistics for many countries, particularly for those in the South. However, it is possible to make a fair estimate since production occurs in a relatively small number of countries and is fairly concentrated on a few species of fish.

In 1989 the total cost of production was estimated at $92.2 billion, excluding capital repayments. Maintenance cost $30 billion, insurance $7 billion, equipment and fishing gear $18.5 billion, and fuel $14 billion. Labour costs, harder to estimate, were around $22.7 billion. The total world revenue from marine fishing, on the other hand, rose to $70 billion. This only equalled the annual running costs for the fleet and did not cover labour costs. The deficit, excluding investment, would be around $22 billion.

The FAO considers this to be a conservative estimate. They point out that the number of fishworkers is almost certainly more than the 13 million referred to in official records. Investment costs and financial charges were not included in the study. The FAO reckons the cost of replacing the fleet as $320 billion. With repayments on capital calculated at another 10 per cent, the annual supplementary cost would amount to $32 billion. This implies a total deficit of $54 billion, pointing to a considerable over-capitalization in global fisheries.

This over-investment is partly the result of massive subsidies which have allowed fleets on the brink of ruin to continue fishing for stocks that have already been overfished. This was the case, in 1989, for fleets from countries in the East, as well as from Europe and Japan. Between 1983 and 1990, the European Union's fisheries public sector aid rose from $80 to $580 million. Of this, more than $200 million went towards financing fisheries agreements, and nearly $100 million were allocated as subsidies for boatbuilding. These figures do not take into account national, regional and local aid.

Annual catches from 1986 to 1992 in different fishing areas (million tonnes)

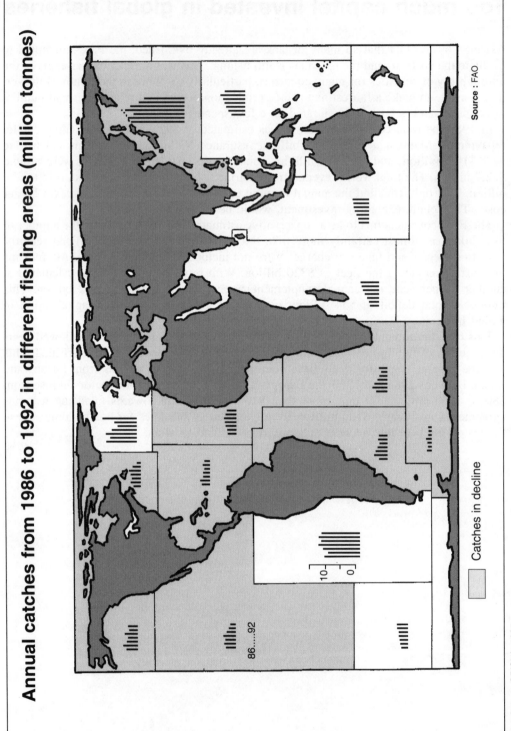

Source : FAO

Catches in decline

86....92

© A Le Sann – CRISLA, 1995

Scarce and highly prized fishery resources

In the past, when a fishery ceased to yield sufficiently large catches, fishing vessels moved on to a different fishing zone, or targeted another species. The sea's fertility seemed to be boundless and its resources inexhaustible. It was not until the end of the nineteenth century that it became apparent that fish stocks are finite, fragile, and extremely vulnerable. Only at the start of the twentieth century did fisheries management become a scientific subject in its own right. It is now vital to the economic, ecological and social future of the fishing industry.

These changes in thinking were accompanied by a growing awareness of the economic importance of the oceans' biological resources. All countries with the means to do so have developed their fishing industries, resulting in a five-fold increase in production over the last 50 years. Total production has risen from 20 million tonnes just after the Second World War, to about 101 million tonnes today. Since the 1970s, however, the growth rate has been declining steadily. Since 1972, it has fallen from 6 per cent per annum to under 2 per cent per annum.

This slowdown can be explained partly by the fact that numerous stocks have been overexploited and partly by the impossibility of re-orienting the fishing industry towards new resources. Excessive fishing has caused many stocks to disappear totally or partially, so much so that it is difficult to draw up a complete list of these lost resources. The FAO has estimated that, in 1993, 69 per cent of global marine fish stocks were already fully or over-exploited. FAO statistics also show a general lowering of catch in many fishing grounds, with the exception of the Indian Ocean and the South-east Pacific. The record total catch figure of 109.6 million tonnes in 1994 was largely due to an unexpected increase in anchovy catches in Peru and Chile.

While ocean resources have been dwindling, global demand for seafood has been steadily rising, as the world population increases and living standards improve. This growing demand has intensified fishing effort and so put even greater pressure on available fish stocks. These different and contradictory developments have created an imbalance between catch capacity and the biological potential of marine populations.

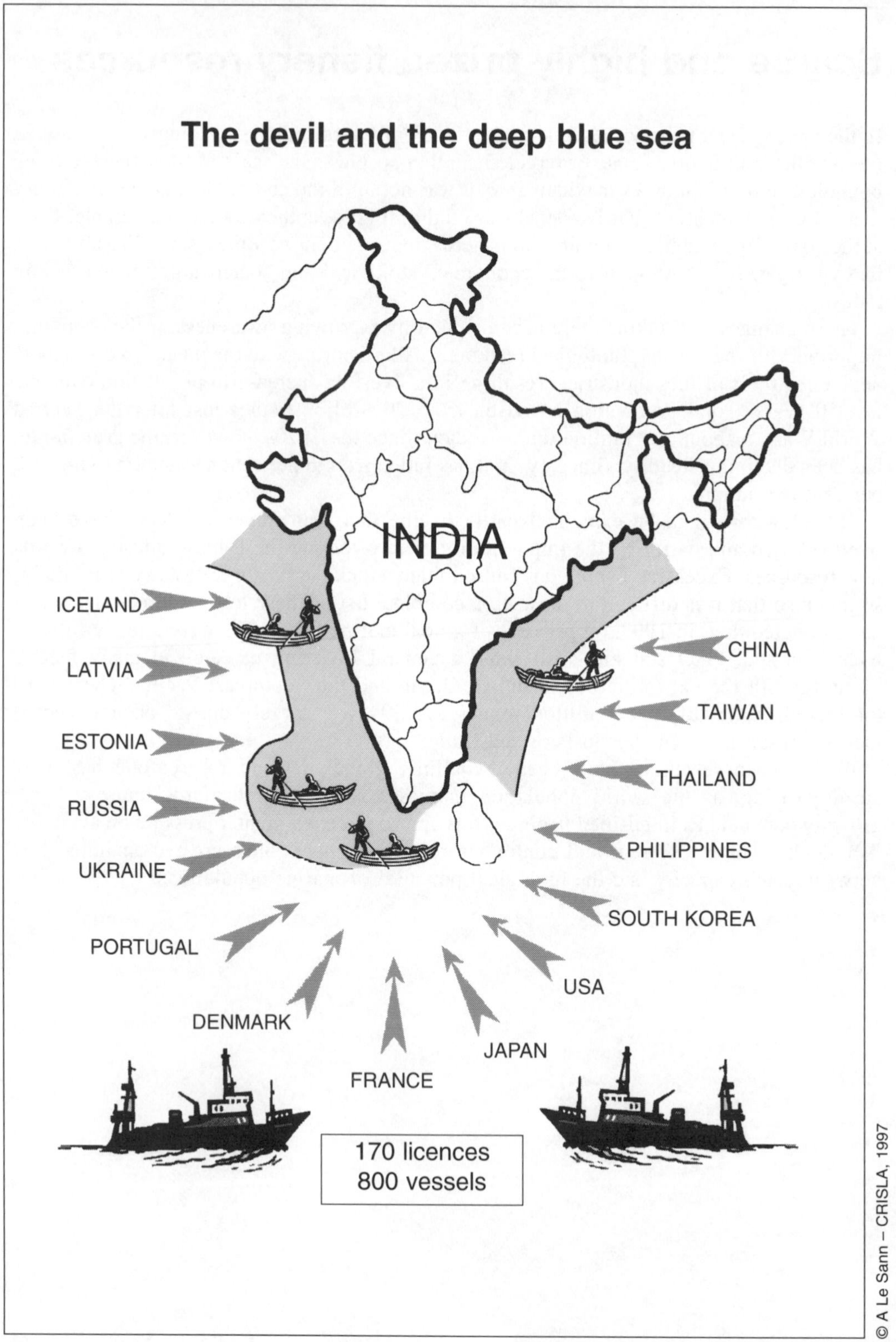

The devil and the deep blue sea

ICELAND

LATVIA

ESTONIA

RUSSIA

UKRAINE

PORTUGAL

DENMARK

FRANCE

JAPAN

USA

SOUTH KOREA

PHILIPPINES

THAILAND

TAIWAN

CHINA

INDIA

170 licences
800 vessels

India gets caught between the devil and the deep blue sea

In 1994, the Government of India announced its intention to open up its 200-mile EEZ to foreign fishing vessels through 'deep-sea joint ventures'. Development of the deep-sea fishing sector formed an integral part of the Government of India's Eighth Five Year Plan. Through its new deep-sea fishing policy, the Ministry of Food Processing was authorized to issue licences to foreign companies to fish in India's deep-sea waters.

These licences were 100 per cent export-oriented, which meant that all the fish caught would be exported, contributing nothing either to the local economy or to local food supplies. Initially, around 170 licences were issued, involving about 800 vessels.

In response, representatives of India's 4.5 million fishermen joined with others, such as the owners of small mechanized boats, to question the role of the Government as the impartial guardian of the public interest. Their response has also demonstrated that it is possible for otherwise conflicting sub-sectors of the fishing community to unite to confront a common threat (see 'Impact of Joint Ventures on Fish Economy', John Kurien, *Economic and Political Weekly*, Bombay, 11 February 1995 and 'Resistance to Multinationals in Indian Waters', John Kurien, *The Ecologist*, Vol. 25, Nos 2/3, 1995).

Past experience with deep-sea fishing in Indian waters and analysis of the resources available show that it is unlikely that such fishing would be profitable. Moreover, deep-sea vessels are likely to encroach into the more productive inshore waters fished by small-scale fisherfolk, overfishing the resource, damaging fishing grounds and running through small boats and gear.

Many of the waters regarded as deep-sea by the Government of India are already fished by the more skilled and adventurous fishermen themselves, without any support or assistance. In fact, a 1992 report by an FAO consultant, commissioned by the Indian government, concluded that deep-sea fishing faced competition from small-scale fishing boats which harvested the resource more effectively (see *Study on the Deep-sea Fisheries Development in India*, M. Guidicelli, FAO, 1992).

Nationwide protests organized by the National Fisheries Action Committee Against Joint Ventures have persuaded the Indian government to reconsider this course of action. While the early reversal of the government's decision on deep-sea joint ventures is unlikely, only a strong, well informed, well organized and well co-ordinated opposition could have achieved such success.

Strong civil and community organizations in India have a long history, dating back to the nineteenth century. More recent examples of campaigns for social reforms are the 'Quit India campaign' of the 1940s, and the pre- and post-Independence movements for social as well as economic development. However, until much more recently, fishing communities had remained on the margins of such movements for social reform.

Post-harvest losses in artisanal fisheries

Transport at sea

Unloading

Storage

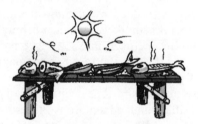

Processing

Transport

Sale

Source : CEASM-CTA, 1986

Post-harvest losses are considerable

A substantial part of the fish catch is lost before it can be consumed. This happens in several ways. Often, a proportion of the catch is thrown back overboard either because it is not profitable to land certain species or because there is no market for them. Some of the catch that is actually landed is lost as a result of problems in regulating temperature during storage and transport. Losses of this kind are especially high in tropical regions. Low-cost processing techniques have been developed by several fishing communities, largely by women. These enable storage for several months. Yet, numerous problems still cause substantial losses. In Africa, these have been estimated to be between 20 and 25 per cent – and sometimes up to 50 per cent – of the catch landed by the artisanal sector. Preventing post-harvest losses therefore has significant potential to raise revenues and food supplies, without intensifying fishing effort.

Procedures to minimize post-harvest losses could be introduced at every stage of the fishing process. Several hours can elapse between capture and landing, during which the fish are unprotected. They can be exposed to the sun in open pirogues (canoes) for four to eight hours, when the fishing is good, and up to 12 hours otherwise. The landing process can also be disastrous for the fish, which are sometimes just left in the sun on the beach. When too many fish are landed, and the market demand cannot absorb the surplus, many are discarded and wasted. In Senegal, for instance, this is undoubtedly a major cause of loss.

Once the fish has been processed, there can be losses in both quantity and quality if the follow-up procedures are unsatisfactory. This could be due to a lack of time, for example, or to lack of funds to purchase salt, fuel, ice or other equipment. Finally, transport conditions, packaging and the time elapsed between capture and sale are all potential sources of losses caused by spoilage and infestation by insects (see *Evaluation des pertes de poisson en Afrique de l'Ouest*, CEASM-CTA, 1986 and *Conserver et transformer le poisson*, CTA-GRET, 1993, p. 290).

Coastal areas under threat

A - Port pollution
B - Domestic refuse from urban areas
C - Heavy metals, chemical waste
D - Refuse resulting from tourism
E - Mining activities (quarries etc.)
F - Outflow from freshwater
    aquaculture farms

G - Pollutants from agricultural
    activity (pesticides etc.)
H - Dam alters coastal hydrology
I - Pig rearing etc.
J - Outflow from marine
    aquaculture installations
L - Deforestation and soil erosion

Source : FAO

© A Le Sann – CRISLA, 1995

Coastal regions under threat

The world's coastal regions have become very densely populated. The people who live here engage in a diversity of activities including industrialization, fishing, aquaculture, transport and tourism. All too often, these exert pressure on the fragile coastal areas and deteriorate coastal ecosystems.

The origins of pollution are often found far away from the coast, for example in the catchments (or watersheds) of rivers. As much as 70 per cent of the pollution of coastal waters arises thus. Agricultural practices, deforestation, and domestic and urban effluents are all contributing factors. According to the UN's Joint Group of Experts on the Scientific Aspects of Marine Pollution (GESAMP), land-based sources account for 44 per cent of marine polution, airborne pollution for 33 per cent (much of it originating on land), dumping of wastes 10 per cent, marine transport 12 per cent, and offshore production 1 per cent (see *The State of the Marine Environment*, GESAMP, 1990).

In coastal regions, mangroves are receding, coral reefs dying and beaches eroding. Marshland areas are silting up and dunes are being destroyed. Sometimes the cause is natural phenomena like storms, but more often than not mankind is the instigator of change, accelerating the actions of natural processes and radically transforming the environment.

It is estimated that, in the Indian Ocean, 25 per cent of pesticides used on land end up in the sea. In 1987, 55 000 tonnes were used on the Indian subcontinent (see M.D. Zingde, *The Siren*, April 1988, pp. 21–24).

In Mauritius, the annual extraction of coral sand is 300 000 tonnes. Of this, 2000 tonnes come from living coral reefs (see *The Siren*, No. 43, 1989).

In the United States, 77 per cent of fish caught are species which depend directly on estuarine environments for their survival (see *Resources mondiales 1992–93*, ed. Frison-Roche, Institut des resources mondiales, Paris, 1992, p. 432).

Between 1965 and 1975, the number of 'red tides' in Japan rose from 44 to 300. Controls imposed on effluents have resulted in a rapid reduction in the number of these phenomena.

The net effect of man's activities on the environment is negative and, most of the time, the degradation of the environment appears to be irreversible (see *Côtes en danger*, R. Paskoff, Masson, Paris, 1993).

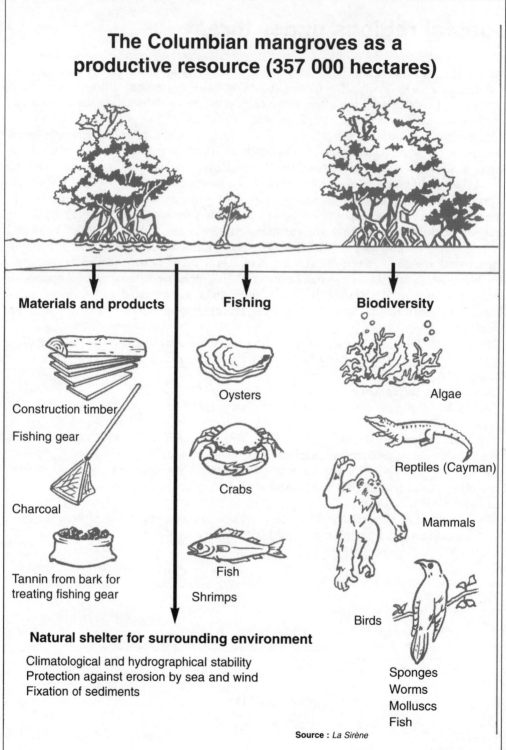

The Columbian mangroves as a productive resource (357 000 hectares)

Materials and products

Construction timber

Fishing gear

Charcoal

Tannin from bark for treating fishing gear

Fishing

Oysters

Crabs

Fish

Shrimps

Biodiversity

Algae

Reptiles (Cayman)

Mammals

Birds

Sponges
Worms
Molluscs
Fish

Natural shelter for surrounding environment

Climatological and hydrographical stability
Protection against erosion by sea and wind
Fixation of sediments

Source : *La Sirène*

Mangroves are in danger

Mangrove forests are ecologically rich environments, found in many coastal areas in tropical and sub-tropical regions. Through them run a myriad of intimately connected life histories. Complex food webs bind mangrove-dwelling life-forms together in a high degree of mutual dependence. Year-round leaf and litter fall provides a continuous supply of nutrients to an ecosystem that contains within it a multitude of aquatic organisms. Alongside the permanent brackish water residents, many kinds of juveniles, particularly young fish and shrimps, find shelter among the mangroves roots and seek out food on the rise and fall of the tide.

Mangroves therefore play a crucial role in coastal ecosystems. They act as filters between land and water, anchoring nutrients and trapping pollutants; they prevent erosion and provide storm protection; they create important nurseries and provide for subsistence farming and fishing activities. It has been estimated that 1 hectare (ha) of mangroves produces an annual yield of 100 kg of fin fish, 25 kg of shrimps, 15 kg of crab meat, 200 kg of molluscs, and 40 kg of sea cucumber in a direct harvest. Indirect harvest of up to 400 kg of fin fish and 75 kg of shrimps that mature elsewhere (see *Our Sea, Our Life*, Lenore Poltan de la Cruz (ed.), VSO, Philippines, 1994).

But mangroves are disappearing rapidly to make way for commercial shrimp farms to meet the ever-increasing global demand. In the Philippines, the mangrove area declined from 450 000 to 145 000 hectares between 1920 and 1988. In Thailand the forest area has shrunk from 290 000 hectares in 1979 to 196 000 hectares today. Much of this decline is the result of the introduction of shrimp farming, the environmental impact of which has been immense. Urbanization and tourist development are other human activities which are having a negative impact on the unique, fragile and crucial mangrove ecosystems.

Other studies have shown that, not including social and ecological services, mangrove ecosystems are economically at par with the most profitable intensive shrimp culture ventures that give net profits in excess of $11,000 per hectare per year (Dr J. Primavera, quoted in *Mangrove Action Project Quarterly News*, June 1995). Therefore, mangrove swamps and forests are not wastelands, but highly productive ecosystems that must be conserved and propagated.

Some efforts are being made to protect mangroves through national parks in Brazil, Malaysia and Bangladesh, for instance. Yet, the proliferation of damaging human activities in coastal areas raises doubts about whether mangroves are likely to survive. An awareness of the importance of mangrove ecosystems has resulted in initiatives by many coastal communities in, for example, Thailand and the Philippines, to undertake replanting programmes.

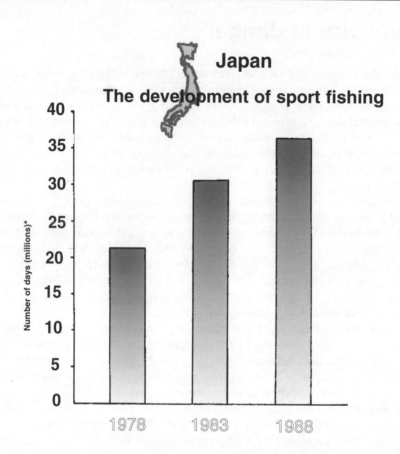

Japan
The development of sport fishing

*Total of days multiplied by the number of amateur fishermen

Professionals and amateurs

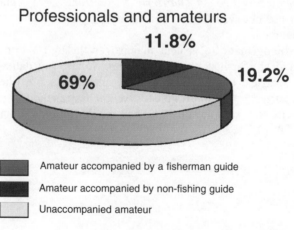

Amateur accompanied by a fisherman guide

Amateur accompanied by non-fishing guide

Unaccompanied amateur

Source : Fishery census

© A Le Sann – CRISLA, 1995

The growth of sport fishing

In many countries of the North and, to a lesser extent, in the South as well, the popularity of sport fishing has increased to such an extent as to cause conflicts between professionals and amateurs. In coastal areas, highly prized species of fish are abundant and are accessible to sports fishermen and other amateurs, and they can exert considerable pressure on fish stocks. In France, spring tides are a time when many shellfish producers complain about raids on their farming areas. Similarly, rod-and-line fishing has a noticeable effect on limited stocks or rare species of fish.

The number of sport fishermen is growing rapidly. In the United States alone, there are 60 million of them and this number is set to rise by 40 per cent by the year 2030. In 1990, these fishermen caught 1.2 million coho salmon (silver salmon). In Great Britain, 38 per cent of salmon caught are fished by non-professionals.

Certain species are threatened more by sport fishermen than by professionals. Studies carried out on the catches of sport fishermen have sometimes yielded extraordinary findings. In Great Britain, the estimated catch in 1987 by 500 000 amateur bass fishermen was between 660 and 700 tonnes, while the professionals landed only 630 tonnes (see *An Appraisal of the UK Bass Fishery and its Management*, MAFF and CEMARE, MAFF Laboratory Leaflet No. 75, 1995).

Given these figures, it is clear that sport fishing should be included within any overall stock management scheme. In Japan, sport fishing is highly developed and falls under the jurisdiction of coastal fishing co-operatives. Servicing sport fishing has become an important sideline business for some professional fishermen, as they provide guidance, lodging and boats for hire. In 1988, 13.6 per cent of fishermen engaged in this as a complementary activity. More than 30 per cent of rod-and-line sport fishermen employ professional guides, although not all guides are fishermen themselves.

While the start of the 1980s saw numerous conflicts between full-time and sport fishermen, sport fishing is now more carefully monitored from within the fishing industry itself. It therefore has the potential to be developed within the co-operative system.

Exclusive Economic Zones (EEZs)

1945		The US claims sovereignty over the continental shelf.
1947	Drawing up of claims	
1948		Chile and Peru lay claim to a 200-mile zone.
		Iceland claims control of fish stocks beyond the 3-mile zone.
1952		Ecuador lays claim to a 200-mile zone.
1958		First United Nations Conference on the Law of the Sea.
1967	Drawing up the convention	Creation of UN committee to manage international waters declared 'Common Heritage of Mankind'.
1973		Caracas: Third Conference on the Law of the Sea. The OAU and the Non-Aligned Movement come out in favour of 200-mile zones.
1977		The US, Canada, China, Australia, EU etc. establish 200-mile exclusive zone.
1982		The adoption of the Convention on the Law of the Sea: 130 votes for, 4 against.
1993	Ratification and preparation of new legislation	60 states ratify the Convention. Negotiations take place at New York on the problem of straddling stocks.
1994		The US ratify the Convention.

EEZ

Territorial waters · 12 · Continental shelf · Straddling stocks · 200 miles · International waters

Source : A. Le Sann

© A Le Sann – CRISLA, 1995

Exclusive Economic Zones take effect

For centuries, fleets from any country were able to fish in the territorial waters of any other country. This freedom of access remained the custom until 1945, when the United States claimed sovereignty over marine resources in part of the Gulf of Mexico. A new concept of the Law of the Sea emerged, under which oceans were to be divided up. This triggered a series of claims being staked. In 1947, Peru enlarged its exclusive fishing zone to 200 miles in order to protect its anchovy grounds. In 1952, other Andean countries followed suit, invoking a Latin American law. Following them, in the 1970s, came other Southern countries and Iceland.

From 1976 onwards, these unilateral decisions led to the generalized concept of Exclusive Economic Zones (EEZs). On 10 December 1982, at Montego Bay, an International Convention on the Law of the Sea was convened to agree upon a principle of 200-mile boundaries delimiting each state's right over fishing grounds (Article 56). In November 1994, after ratification by over 60 states, the United Nations Convention on the Law of the Sea (UNCLOS) became international law.

An EEZ corresponds to a zone extending 188 nautical miles beyond the 12 nautical miles of territorial waters that border the coast of each country and over which the country has sovereign rights for exploration, exploitation, conservation and management of natural resources, biological or mineral. In fishing terms, this translates into the appropriation of stocks by the coastal state. Fishing fleets from other countries have to comply with the host country's regulations, paying fishing duties or taxes and respecting the quotas imposed. The coastal state can, in turn, take whatever measures it deems necessary to enforce its own laws, such as boarding and inspecting vessels, imposing monitoring standards and imprisoning offenders.

Today, however, the 188-mile limit is being challenged by the sensitive problem of straddling stocks. This could lead to the extension of EEZs. Some countries, Canada for example, would support such an extension.

It seems that the 1982 Montego Bay Convention resolution to create an international body to manage resources of fish, mineral reserves and oil in international waters, and thereby protect the interests of the South, has been forgotten. The resistance of industrialized countries, particularly the United States, has sidelined these good intentions. Today, the more powerful nations still hold sway over international waters (see 'The Devil and the Deep Blue Sea', *Down to Earth*, November 1994).

The dispute over drift-nets and tuna fishing

	France	Spain	Ecologists
Before 1970	Pole and line fishing		
1970s and 1980s	Albacore fishing ceases due to low revenue. Rise in tropical tuna fishing using purse-seiners.	Pole and line activity continues.	Emergence of environmental protection organizations.
End of the 1980s and early 1990s	New technique: drift-nets and mid-water or pelagic trawling. Partial recovery in albacore production in France.	Crisis in industry due to low revenues, low productivity, and competition from the French.	Environmentalists oppose seine fishing in the East Pacific and the use of drift-nets worldwide due to threat posed to dolphins.
The state of play in 1994	Limits on length of nets (1 km per crew member) accepted by fishermen. Possibility of net fishing at night, and line fishing by day. Nets considered selective posing no major threat to mammals.	Fishermen reject drift-nets, but using line fishing does not solve the problem of low revenue.	The use of drift-nets is totally condemned, but the problem of low revenue is not addressed.

Source : A. Le Sann

Environmental groups turn on the pressure

During the 1980s, environmental protection groups emerged as major players on the world's fisheries scene. Sometimes they ally with fishermen, as, for example, in the fight against pollution. At other times, they support one side against another; for example, in the Bay of Biscay, where Greenpeace supported the Spanish, who fish tuna with lines, against the French, who use nets.

Often, these environmental groups condemn certain fishing methods and, as follow-up acts, disrupt the market or urge for the boycott of products thus caught. The most spectacular of their campaigns concerned the tuna seiners in the Pacific which killed thousands of dolphins caught in the purse seines used to fish tuna. The Japanese and the Taiwanese fished tuna with 'wall of death' drift-nets, tens of kilometres long, which caught many other species too. By organizing the boycott of tuna caught with such gear, the environmental groups scored points with the American tuna seiners. With the support of countries in the South Pacific, they have managed to obtain a United Nations resolution prohibiting the use of drift-nets over 2.5 km in length on the high seas. Also in the USA, a strong move to ban the imports of tropical prawns is under way, as certain kinds of shrimp trawlers capture turtles along with the prawns, thus endangering the survival of several species of turtle.

On 22 February 1996, Unilever and the World Wide Fund for Nature (WWF) signed a key agreement to set up a Marine Stewardship Council to encourage responsible codes of fishing practice that respect ocean resources. The Council initiative will also be responsible for developing and implementing a system of 'eco-labels' to identify environment-friendly fish produce. From the year 2005 onwards, Unilever will buy only fish bearing such labels. Unilever has also decided to stop buying fish oils derived from non-sustainable industrial fishing in European waters.

Clearly, environmental groups will increasingly play a vital role in fisheries policies. Fishworkers should thus learn to negotiate and work with them, even if their vision of the sea is somewhat different from their own. Dolphins, for instance, are perceived by fishermen as competitors or potential destroyers of nets, and not as the friendly swimming companions seen on television.

For their part, the environmental groups – whose point of view should be given due consideration – would do well to stop imposing dictates (as some do) and, instead, look more closely at the social, economic and cultural realities of fishing communities the world over.

Sustainability is as much about conserving fish stocks as it is about sustaining fishing as a livelihood in fishing communities with access to few other resources. Linking and rationalizing environmental and socio-economic concerns is crucial, given the context of increasing centralization, globalization and diminishing employment opportunities in small coastal communities.

Ecoprotection or barriers to trade?

USA

Protection of commercial interests in USA

1988
Marine Mammal
Protection Act

Protection
of dolphins

Tuna embargo on the
import of yellow fin tuna
from Mexico

Tuna fleet
reduction
85 boats to 54

Economic losses in Mexico
US$500 millions

Tuna exports
declining by 70%

30 000 jobs lost

90% increase
in domestic
consumption

New export
markets
in Asia and
Europe

MEXICO

Environmental laws: ecoprotection or barriers to trade?

In many areas, fishermen use the age-old practice of locating shoals of tuna by searching for dolphins, having observed that some tuna often swim with dolphins. In US, Mexican and many other fisheries, this practice did not endanger dolphins before the late 1950s, as the main tuna harvesting technique used was 'pole and line'. The development of the purse seine enabled fishing boats to surround the dolphins and tuna completely with their nets, a technique which has caused the death of millions of dolphins – caught and drowned in the nets along with the tuna.

American consumers and interest groups which promote environmental issues have been instrumental in influencing US trade laws and fishing regulations. The US government has placed embargoes on imports of fish of particular species, and of species caught by particular fishing methods or from particular sea areas. US fishermen have now devised methods of minimizing dolphin deaths, either by allowing their escape before hauling in the nets, or by switching to other types of gear.

The Marine Mammal Protection Act (MMPA) is designed to protect marine mammals from human activities, including fishing. Under the MMPA, amended in 1988, the importation of yellow fin tuna to the USA has to comply with two main provisions: the level of dolphin mortality caused by the fishing operation has to be similar to that of the USA, and an intermediary country importing tuna to the USA must prove that this complies with the US restrictions.

In 1990, under these provisions, the USA imposed an embargo on the import of yellow fin tuna from Mexico, claiming that the Mexican manner of harvesting yellow fin tuna (mainly by purse seine) resulted in levels of dolphin death above the standards set by the MMPA. Mexico, a member of the General Agreement on Tariffs and Trade (GATT) since 1986, complained that the US tuna embargo was inconsistent with the provisions of GATT. They claimed that Mexican fishworkers were attempting to comply with the requirements of the MMPA, that the fishing activities were taking place in international or Mexican waters (i.e. non-US waters), and that Mexican fishworkers were not breaching any Mexican or international law concerning either tuna harvesting or dolphin protection.

In 1991, the GATT adjudication panel found in favour of Mexico. However, Mexico did not actively pursue the case because of their fear of jeopardizing the impending conclusion with the USA of the North American Free Trade Agreement (NAFTA) and the political outcry in the USA caused by the 1991 GATT panel decision.

The US tuna embargo has inflicted considerable economic damage on Mexico's tuna industry, estimated at US$500 million. Mexican tuna interests are pushing for the embargo to be lifted, but at the same time intensifying efforts to find export markets in other parts of the world, such as Asia and Europe (see *World Fishing*, Vol. 46 No.2, February 1997).

Spain's many fish wars

British Isles

France

Canada

Spain

Namibia

Morocco

Algeria

Conflicts over gear

Resource conflicts

Conflicts over access rights

1000 boats fishing in European waters

1140 in the rest of the world, with 650 in Moroccan waters

Source : D. Cadio

© A Le Sann – CRISLA, 1995

Conflicts erupt more and more frequently

Conflicts over fishing grounds are not new. They have always occurred but, since the Exclusive Economic Zones (EEZs) were established in the 1970s, disputes have become more frequent and more violent than ever before. Due to the establishment of EEZs, access to the world's oceans has been radically re-organized and the access rights of foreign fishing vessels have been curtailed. Negotiations, international fisheries agreements (such as those between European and African countries) and recourse to an international tribunal (as, for example, in the case of the Franco–Canadian conflict) have sometimes succeeded in resolving conflicts.

More often than not, however, foreign boats are expelled from territorial waters and EEZs by force. Vessels are boarded and crew imprisoned, as in the 1992 Spanish–Namibian conflict. Even weapons were used in 1994 against Spanish boats in French, Irish and Portuguese waters and, in 1991, in Algerian waters. Since then, conflicts over limits to fishing grounds have been most intense in Asia. For instance, fights have broken out between Vietnam and Cambodia, and between China and Vietnam. Thousands of Thai fishermen have also landed in jail because of illegal fishing.

While sovereignty issues are generally at the root of such conflicts, they are also the manifestation of competition for access to fish stocks, in coastal waters as much as on the high seas. In addition, the use of flags of convenience serves to exacerbate the problem. The country where a boat is registered does not necessarily identify its country of its origin, and enables fishing companies to flout international fishing and labour conventions with impunity.

Tensions are also aggravated by conflicts between users of different techniques. The right to use passive fishing equipment like nets, long-lines and fish traps is often contested by those who use active gear like trawls and seine-nets, because such equipment often gets caught and carried off by trawlers.

Though conflicts are often ecological or social in nature, they ultimately divide artisanal and industrial fishermen. In India, for instance, artisanal fishermen have lately been very vociferous in condemning shrimp trawlers whose fishing methods jeopardize fish stocks. In this type of conflict, where industrial fisheries often enjoy the benefits of state aid, negotiating a solution can be very difficult, as it involves working across totally different social and economic sectors.

Consultations among fishermen serve to reduce conflict. At Kayar, in Senegal, for instance, a local fishing committee was created which has managed to resolve a very long-standing feud between local and migrant fishermen.

In the UK, the 'Save Britain's Fish' campaign has been welcomed by certain parts of the industry. The campaign calls for the UK to leave the Common Fisheries Policy, and establishing a UK EEZ. It is also of national concern that some 30 per cent of British catches are made by so-called 'quota hoppers', UK-registered vessels manned by Dutch and Spanish crews (see 'Britain's Fishing Industry and the EU Common Fisheries Policy', Simon Fairlie, *The Ecologist* Vol. 25 No. 2/3, 1995).

Blue Europe
(Common Fisheries Policy – CFP)

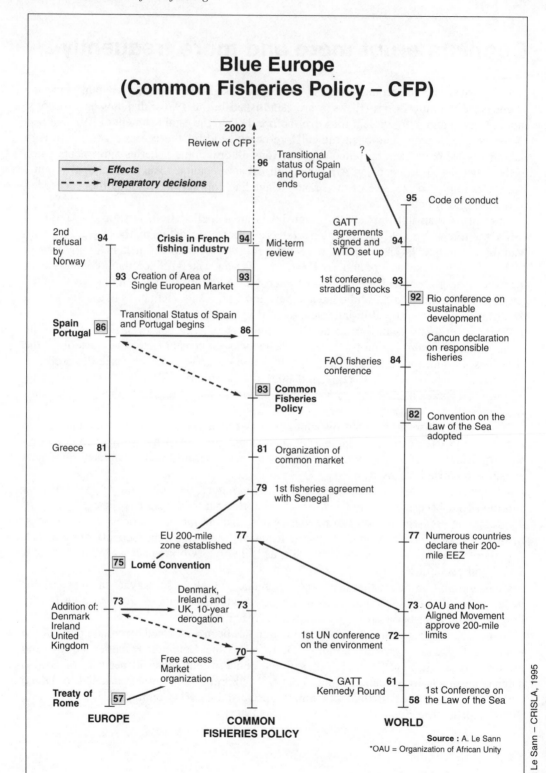

2002
Review of CFP

→ **Effects**
--→ **Preparatory decisions**

96 Transitional status of Spain and Portugal ends

?

95 Code of conduct

2nd refusal by Norway 94   **Crisis in French fishing industry** 94 Mid-term review

GATT agreements signed and WTO set up 94

93 Creation of Area of Single European Market 93

1st conference straddling stocks 93

92 Rio conference on sustainable development

Spain Portugal 86   Transitional Status of Spain and Portugal begins 86

Cancun declaration on responsible fisheries

FAO fisheries conference 84

83 **Common Fisheries Policy**

82 Convention on the Law of the Sea adopted

Greece 81   81 Organization of common market

79 1st fisheries agreement with Senegal

EU 200-mile zone established 77   77 Numerous countries declare their 200-mile EEZ

75 **Lomé Convention**

Addition of: Denmark Ireland United Kingdom 73   Denmark, Ireland and UK, 10-year derogation 73   73 OAU and Non-Aligned Movement approve 200-mile limits

1st UN conference on the environment 72

Free access Market organization 70

GATT Kennedy Round 61

Treaty of Rome 57   1st Conference on the Law of the Sea 58

EUROPE   **COMMON FISHERIES POLICY**   **WORLD**

Source : A. Le Sann
*OAU = Organization of African Unity

© A Le Sann – CRISLA, 1995

Blue Europe is a huge market

The Treaty of Rome, signed in 1957, led to the development of a European common market, which included seafood. Initially fisheries were dealt with under the Common Agricultural Policy, and it was not until 1983 that a separate Common Fisheries Policy, otherwise known as 'Blue Europe', was established. The co-ordination and management of fisheries, a diverse and fragmented sector, has posed many problems for the European Union (EU). Growing membership and constant change in the EU has added to the problems.

Paradoxically, the establishment of EEZs on a global basis has speeded up the process of establishing a common market in the EU. While the practices of larger fishing powers have been disrupted, an EEZ (excluding the Mediterranean) where only members' vessels could fish came into existence on 1 January 1977. Russian and Eastern European factory ships were excluded, as was the impressive Spanish armada. Only those vessels with licences granted by Brussels were allowed to fish. Finally, on 25 January 1983, an agreement on community fishing regulations led to the formulation of the Common Fisheries Policy for the ten States which were then members of the EU.

In 1986, Portugal and Spain joined the EU, but were denied equal fishing rights because of the size of their fleets. The Spanish felt that the restrictions imposed on them were discriminatory. This complaint has often been at the root of violent confrontations between Spanish or Basque fishermen on one side, and French, English and Irish fishermen on the other.

Apart from the problems of regulating access to available resources, there also exists an enormous disparity in social conditions and incomes between some of the countries. While Blue Europe has succeeded in creating a single market, its management of fish stocks has been a failure. Very few attempts have been made to reconcile the national and regional differences in social conditions and working conditions.

Significantly, the EU has a considerable catch potential (4.8 million tonnes, in 1992, for the 12 EU countries, which represents 5 per cent of the world production figure for fish). Above all, the EU is the world's biggest market for seafood – Europe's 350 million inhabitants consume 28.7 kg of seafood per person per year and the EU imports $16.6 billion worth of seafood, which is 36 per cent of the total world trade. However, being both divided and obsessed by the need to satisfy its ever growing demands, the EU has until now not been able to reach any collective agreement on how to exert concerted pressure to change the existing economic order in the global fishing industry in its favour.

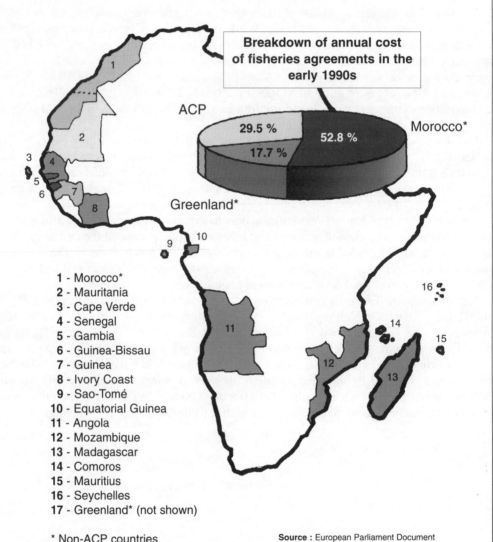

Who benefits from fisheries agreements between the EU and third countries?

Breakdown of annual cost of fisheries agreements in the early 1990s

ACP

Morocco*

29.5 %

52.8 %

17.7 %

Greenland*

1 - Morocco*
2 - Mauritania
3 - Cape Verde
4 - Senegal
5 - Gambia
6 - Guinea-Bissau
7 - Guinea
8 - Ivory Coast
9 - Sao-Tomé
10 - Equatorial Guinea
11 - Angola
12 - Mozambique
13 - Madagascar
14 - Comoros
15 - Mauritius
16 - Seychelles
17 - Greenland* (not shown)

* Non-ACP countries

Source : European Parliament Document

© A. Le Sann – CRISLA, 1995

Fisheries agreements have a commercial bias

In 1976, anticipating the introduction of EEZs, the EU (or European Economic Community – EEC, as it was then called) initiated its first fisheries agreements with non-EEC states. Initially these were an important means of maintaining access to the distant waters traditionally fished by member states' vessels, but which had extended their fishing zones to 200 miles. Today, the rationale for such agreements has been expanded to include the maintenance of fish supplies to the EU, as a means of supporting European fishing industries and of reducing the number of fishing vessels on the EU register. This 'export of excess fishing capacity' has become one of the key elements of EU fisheries policy to maintain a balance within the EU fishing industry (between resources available, catching capacity, and national interests).

So far there are about 25 agreements (14 of which are with countries in Africa and the Indian Ocean), permitting around 4000 European vessels to fish in zones outside the EU. Of these, about 300 are licensed to fish in the EEZs of ACP countries, where the Lomé Convention provides a framework and policy guidelines for EU fisheries agreements. All fisheries agreements with ACP countries are of the 'cash for access' type (now called 'First Generation' agreements), whereby the state in question grants fishing rights to EU vessels in return for financial compensation and market access from the EU. Many of these agreements also feature a technical and scientific co-operation component.

The European Fisheries Commission argues that fisheries agreements are mutually beneficial commercial arrangements. The EU gains access to fish stocks that are surplus to the requirements of the coastal state, and the coastal state receives compensation. However, in many cases it is far from certain that there is a surplus. Rather than 'compensation', the payment made by the EU is an economic inducement to the coastal state to allow the EU fishing access. As such, compensation is used by the EU negotiators as an economic lever, and effectively represents a significant subsidy to its distant water fleets.

While the Lomé Convention highlights the importance of development co-operation, commercial and financial considerations have predominated in fisheries agreements (see *La Politique commune des Pêches*, M. Ould El Kettab, CRISLA, 1995). There is therefore a contradiction between what the EU espouses in its policies for development co-operation, and what it practises through its fisheries agreements.

Although 20 years have passed since these fisheries agreements were first negotiated, not much data is available for any satisfactory evaluation of their impacts. Meanwhile, the possibilities for re-deploying the EU's surplus fishing capacity in ACP countries appear to be dwindling. The First Generation agreements have come in for much criticism. Under arrangements in Second Generation agreements (as with Argentina), vessels from the EU register can be transferred to the register of the partner country. These have the effect of transferring the problem of the idle tonnage from the EU to other countries. The EU is now developing new Third Generation accords, based on joint ventures, which are also likely to involve the transfer of vessels from the European register to the partner country register (as is being discussed with South Africa and Namibia). This does not, however, fundamentally alter the outcome of such agreements. Commercial considerations still predominate.

Aquaculture vs. capture fisheries

Farmed bass

Wild bass

Advantages

- Planned regular supply
- Size suited to market demand
- Low production cost
- Mass production

- Wild product
- Better quality, less fat
- Absence of medicinal residues

Disadvantages

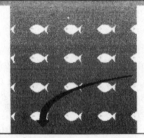

- Intensive culture results in pollution
- Feed derived from fishmeal (wasteful of protein)
- Medication required
- Product is devalued

- Irregular unpredictable supply
- High cost
- Irregular size not always adapted to customers' requirements

Source : *Le Marin.* Hors-série, December 1994.

Aquaculture competes in the market for fish

The increasing growth of intensive aquaculture for fish and shellfish, which burst onto the scene in the 1980s, is likely to include an ever-increasing number of new species. Modern aquaculture is dedicated mainly to producing high-value species for luxury markets in order to ensure decent profit margins from intensively managed operations.

However, rapid increases in production have lowered prices and forced farmed fish down-market. In some cases this has caused a total market collapse. The market repercussions can be devastating for the same or similar wild caught fish. For example, in France the average selling price of fresh salmon has fallen from FF50 per kg in 1983 to FF30 per kg in 1993. Massive imports of salmon (80 000 tonnes into France in 1993) have affected the market for white fish, although the consumption of salmon has spread to people who do not usually eat fish.

In Europe, the same market phenomenon has been seen in the aquaculture for sea bass, which produced less than 1000 tonnes in 1987, and an estimated 25 000 tonnes in 1994. French production of farmed sea bass rose from 1040 tonnes in 1992 to nearly 2000 tonnes in 1993. In Greece, fish farms produce more than 8000 tonnes of bass and sea bream. This has depressed the wholesale price of bass, which has declined by 24 per cent since 1991 (see *An Appraisal of the UK Bass Fishery and its Management*, MAFF and CEMARE, MAFF Laboratory Leaflet No. 75, 1995).

Norway's production capacity for salmon is 750 000 tonnes. At the moment production increases have been halted because the market is saturated. Producers are considering the option of producing white salmon (without pigmentation) and letting this compete in the market for white fish.

The strength of aquaculture is that it allows fish to be produced according to demand. In theory, market supply can be controlled and quality maintained uniformly. Consumers should also be informed whether the fish they are buying is farmed or wild. The quality varies greatly between the two, even if it is difficult to tell the difference by taste alone. Farmed fish tend to be more fatty and have usually been vaccinated or have received medication.

Evidently, great vigilance is needed, as the markets for species such as sea bream and turbot will increasingly be affected by aquaculture. To maintain their market niche, wild caught fish will have to prove their superior quality, improve their image, and develop new marketing strategies.

Meanwhile, an encouraging sign is that, in 1994, the farmed and wild sea bass markets evolved in perceptibly different ways, as if for two entirely different products. This lends hope that markets for the wild product will survive (see *Le Marin*, Special Edition, December 1994, p. 12).

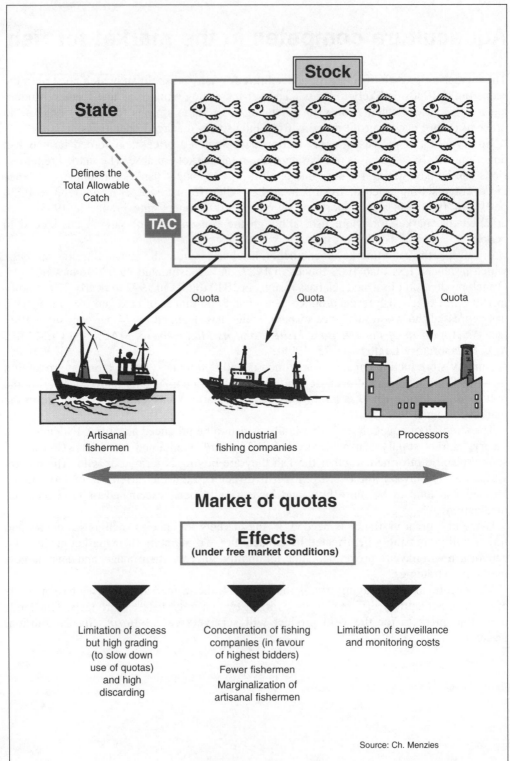

Source: Ch. Menzies

Individual Transferable Quotas (ITQ)

Open access has been cited as one of the main causes of fish stock depletion. Many fisheries managers are therefore advocating the introduction of private property regimes into fisheries to restrict access.

The development of quota management has given rise to the concept of transferable quotas, which allocates quotas through a market mechanism. In New Zealand a system known as 'Individual Transferable Quotas' (ITQs) was introduced in the early 1980s. With ITQs, fish quotas are effectively sold off to the highest bidder. There are at least two underlying assumptions of the ITQ system that make it particularly attractive to fisheries managers:

- The real market price is paid for the access to fish stocks. Quotas are sold to the highest bidder, with the revenues accruing to the state. These revenues can help to cover the costs of monitoring and regulating the fishery.
- Ownership of fish stocks by fishing companies will lead to enlightened self-interest. If fishworkers and fishing companies hold private property rights in fish stocks, they will have a long-term stake in maintaining the stocks at healthy levels.

One of the principal drawbacks of ITQs is that quotas can accumulate in the hands of a few large businesses. Today's fishworkers can sell off the livelihood rights of future generations – thereby disenfranchising communities that have a tradition of fishing.

In Canada's west-coast halibut fishery, a management system based on transferable vessel quotas has been in force since the early 1990s. The Individual Vessel Quota (IVQ) system is quite different from the ITQ system of New Zealand. Benefits include increased value of fish landings (higher ex-vessel prices) and higher earnings for the crew members. However, the IVQ system decreases job security for crew members, as quotas are owned by the vessel owner, and has been cited as the cause of job losses in Canada.

Elsewhere in British Columbia, quotas are allocated according to a formula based on a calculated 'Total Allowable Catch' (TAC). While the proportion of the TAC allocated to quota-holding vessels remains the same, the actual quota will vary as the TAC varies. This provides some stability and parity between licence holders.

Although there is some restriction on the accumulation of quotas by any vessel, there are no restrictions on how much quota an individual or corporation may own. As a consequence many small communities in British Columbia are suffering as licences are bought up by outsiders, and fish processing firms become more centralized and based in the larger urban centres (see 'Closed Competition', Leith Duncan, *The Ecologist*, Vol. 25, No. 2/3, 1995).

SECTION 3

WHAT NEEDS TO
BE DONE

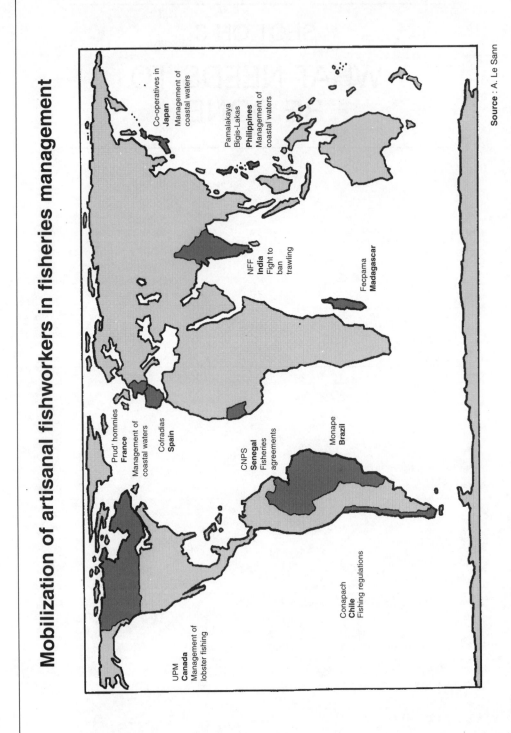

Mobilization of artisanal fishworkers in fisheries management

Co-operatives in
Japan
Management of
coastal waters

Pamalakaya
Bigis-Lakas
Philippines
Management of
coastal waters

NFF
India
Fight to
ban
trawling

Fecpama
Madagascar

Prud' hommies
France
Management of
coastal waters

Cofradias
Spain

CNPS
Senegal
Fisheries
agreements

Monape
Brazil

UPM
Canada
Management of
lobster fishing

Conapach
Chile
Fishing regulations

Source : A. Le Sann

Artisanal fishworkers must be organized

Traditionally, fishing communities were organized around the management of fishing expeditions. Communities have developed regulations according to their fishing practices (kinds of gear used, fishing seasons, sharing the catch, and so on). Such rules have enabled communities not only to survive for centuries, but also to manage the process of technical innovation (to adopt, adapt or reject new technologies). See 'Overfishing: Causes and consequences', *The Ecologist*, Vol. 25, Nos. 2–3, March 1995.

Today, however, these communities are under threat and their social structures have been disrupted by modernization. New players from outside the community have become involved, new social divisions have appeared, and relations between the different generations are changing. The proliferation of technical innovations is often beyond the control of the community itself, and markets are becoming increasingly global.

Not surprisingly, these traditional communities now find themselves marginalized by new and powerful interests involved in the management of the fishing industry – multinational companies, governments, scientists, and environmental groups. The net result is that they can no longer make themselves heard or protect their own interests.

For example, in 1984 the FAO organized the World Conference on Fisheries Management and Development in Rome to draw up a global fishing strategy within the context of the new international Law of the Sea. However, they omitted to include representation or dialogue with fishworker organizations. This prompted Indian fishworkers and several NGOs to organize a parallel conference for professional fishworker organizations. This led to the establishment of the ICSF (International Collective in Support of Fishworkers), which encourages and supports the formation and interaction of artisanal fishworker organizations all over the world.

Thousands of fishworkers have come together to form organizations in India, the Philippines, Senegal, Madagascar and Brazil, strong enough to be able to negotiate with governments, environmental groups and scientific bodies. Networks spanning continents are gradually forming. Paradoxically enough, France, a pioneer in the field of organization, has been backward in this area – it was only in 1993 that a French Fishermen's Survival Committee was formed.

It is absolutely vital to restore the role of fishworkers and their communities in resource management, and that their access rights and rights to participate in their own development are upheld. However, organization is hampered by the fact that fishing communities may themselves be divided socially and economically. Yet, only by organization can power be restored to fishworkers and only thus can be created the conditions necessary for the rational management of fish stocks and the marine environment.

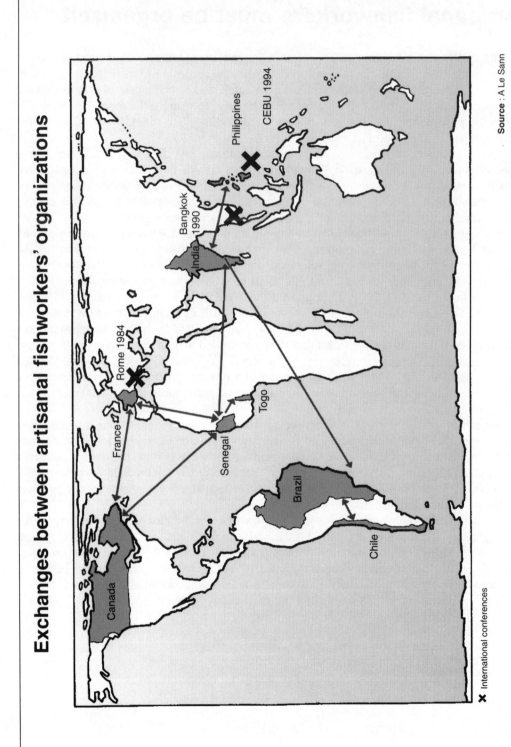

Exchanges between artisanal fishworkers' organizations

✖ International conferences

Source : A Le Sann

© A Le Sann – CRISLA, 1995

The need for international co-operation

In fisheries, development co-operation has often failed. Sometimes it has even aggravated crises in the very fishing communities it was supposed to be helping. In the 1960s, for instance, an Indo-Norwegian programme, which initiated trawling for prawns in India's coastal waters, ended up fuelling the nation's export drive and serving capitalists from outside the traditional fishing communities. In other cases, programmes failed because they ultimately succeeded only in reinforcing government control over the sector.

On the other hand, fishing communities themselves are well able to adapt new techniques to suit their own interests with the minimum of development aid. This has happened, for example, in the case of motorization of traditional fishing vessels. In Senegal, the use of purse-seine nets spread rapidly during the 1970s, with very little technical support.

It is vital, therefore, to encourage exchanges among all fishworkers – men as well as women – who can readily identify how other practices can be relevant and adaptable to their own technical and organizational needs, interests and capabilities.

NGOs have a central role to play in making the necessary contacts and in establishing international networks. Decisions concerning fishworkers – whether on fisheries agreements, the Law of the Sea or on fishing gear regulations – are too often made outside national frameworks. It is therefore vital to encourage the formation of organizations in every country able to represent fishworkers internationally and help them participate in decision-making processes. Several NGOs, such as CCFD and ICSF, have enlisted the support of EU fishworkers to help fishworkers from Senegal to participate and voice their concerns during the negotiation of fisheries agreements between the EU and Senegal in 1992, 1994 and 1996.

Fishworkers from the Philippines, France, India, Senegal and Chile participated in the development of the FAO's Code of Conduct for Responsible Fisheries as part of the ICSF delegation. During the negotiations at the UN Conference on Straddling Fish Stocks and Highly Migratory Fish Stocks in New York, several fishworkers' organizations, supported by NGOs and environmental groups, were able to influence the drafting of the final document. Such exchanges have recently led to the mooting of a World Council of Professional Fish Harvesters.

How women's role is evolving

Women in the traditional community ...

Pre-capture	Capture	Processing	Sales

... and in the context of a modern fishing economy

Pre-capture	Capture	Industrial processing	Sales

Source : A Le Sann

Women's roles must be recognized

Within the fishing industry, modernization has often marginalized women and deprived them of their livelihood. In India, for example, the use of synthetic factory-made nets in preference to locally woven ones has cost thousands of women their jobs.

Modernization has also led to the landing of fish catches in distant ports rather than on beaches where women traditionally participated in post-harvest activities. Once the activity becomes port-centred, the scale of activity becomes tremendously enlarged. It is then necessary to purchase larger quantities of fish and transport them over longer distances – for which access to lorries is vital. All this calls for much larger amounts of capital than most women possess or could possibly put together. In countries of the North, the equivalent phenomenon might be the displacement of the boat-owners' wives, who traditionally shared in the administration of the business, by co-operative management groups.

The role of women is far from secondary. In times of crisis, they often play a decisive role, as in France in 1993 and 1994, when fishermen's wives mobilized to help their striking men. In India, at the start of the 1980s, women participated vigorously in the fight to resist trawling. The National Fishworkers' Forum in India has set up a training programme for both women and men, which aims to integrate women at all levels of management in fisheries. In Senegal, the CNPS (the National Collective of Senegalese Artisanal Fishermen) has encouraged the setting up of active women's groups.

Normally, however, women fight to defend the interests of fishworkers in general, rather than to further their own interests. Yet, even though they represent an important part of the militant grassroots movement, they do not usually have access to key management positions within associations. Moreover, they often find themselves increasingly subjected to bureaucratization. This is unfortunate, since women can play a vital role in bringing fresh dynamism to organizations – old or new, and whichever country they are situated in.

A fishing village in the Philippines takes the initiative in environmental restoration

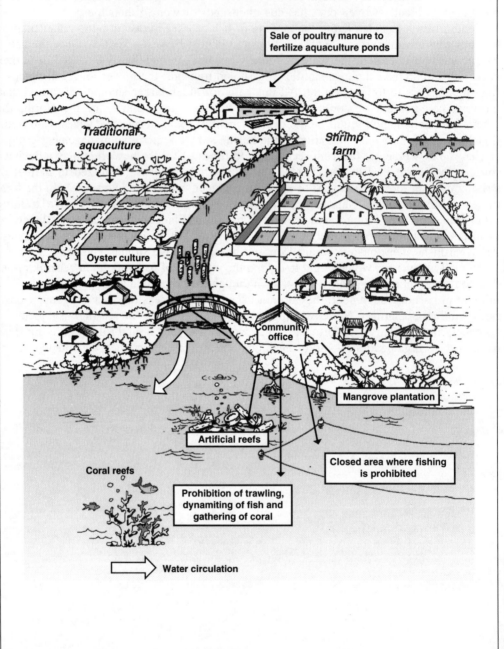

Sale of poultry manure to fertilize aquaculture ponds

Traditional aquaculture

Shrimp farm

Oyster culture

Community office

Mangrove plantation

Artificial reefs

Closed area where fishing is prohibited

Coral reefs

Prohibition of trawling, dynamiting of fish and gathering of coral

Water circulation

The environment must be protected

If the remaining natural resources of the world are to be preserved and, with them, the conditions which will allow regeneration of coastal and marine life, it is essential to have enforceable policies for environmental protection.

While coastlines are the most productive areas, they are also often the most fragile and most threatened. Remedial action is needed both on land and at sea. River catchments (or watersheds) are an obvious target for stringent controls, since rivers transport pollutants seawards, where they accumulate. However, the diversity of the coastal fringe means that not all zones are equally productive or equally fragile. Priorities have to be set.

Dams in the north-west of the United States have been destroyed to allow salmon to return to their breeding grounds. An Environmental Impact Assessment study confirmed that the construction of a dam resulted in more loss than gain (see *Fishing News International*, May 1994). Scientists and fishworkers estimate that, without including Alaska, it should be possible to double fish catches if the estuarine marshlands and the rivers are restored to their original ecological state.

Marshlands in temperate regions and mangroves in tropical regions play an indispensable role in maintaining the biological richness of marine life. Many fishing communities have initiated projects to replant and restore them. A French research study showed that 400 hectares of saltwater marshland supplies nutrients for a marine area of 3400 hectares.

In many countries, shellfish farming, which could be a source of abundant and inexpensive protein, has been hindered by water pollution which inhibits the growth of farmed species and makes the final produce impossible to sell. For example, TBT (tri-butyl tin) is often used in an anti-fouling paint for boats. TBT is highly toxic for marine life, destroys plankton, prevents the growth of oyster and mussel larvae, causes infertility in whelks, and deforms bones in farmed fish. It is hardly surprising, therefore, that many countries have now banned the use of paints containing TBT.

Undoubtedly, the most urgent priority today is to protect and restore the environmental basis of productivity in the oceans. The destruction of coral reefs, for instance, must be stopped. If necessary, artificial reefs should be constructed to rehabilitate the environment and provide fish habitats.

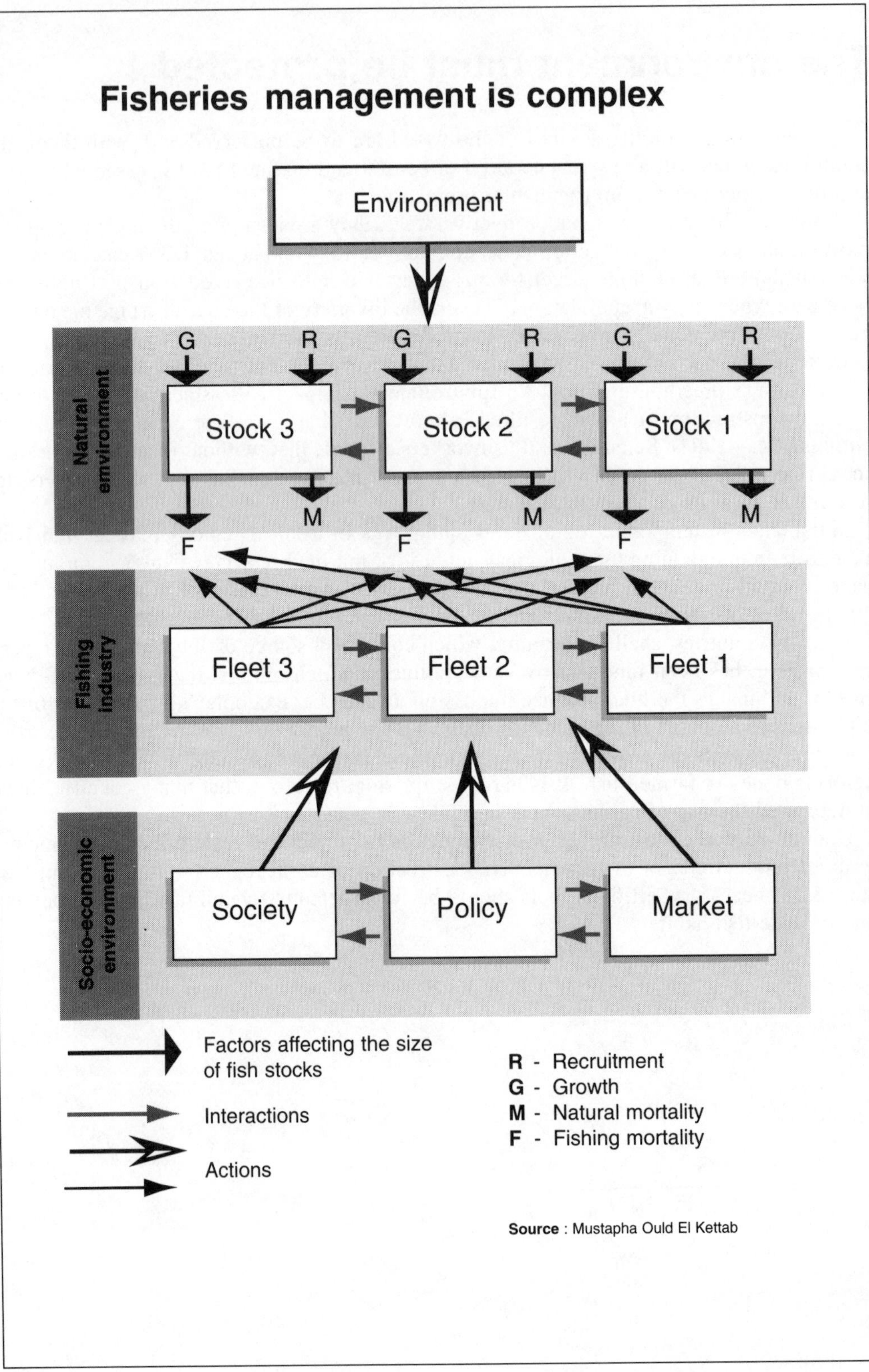

Fisheries management is complex

Environment

Natural environment

| G | R | G | R | G | R |

Stock 3 → Stock 2 → Stock 1

M   M   M

F   F   F

Fishing industry

Fleet 3 → Fleet 2 → Fleet 1

Socio-economic environment

Society → Policy → Market

➤ Factors affecting the size of fish stocks

→ Interactions

➤ Actions

➤ Actions

R - Recruitment
G - Growth
M - Natural mortality
F - Fishing mortality

Source : Mustapha Ould El Kettab

© A Le Sann – CRISLA, 1995

Highly complex systems must be managed well

The regulation of fishing activities is based largely on theoretical models developed at the beginning of the twentieth century. These were constructed around ecological concepts such as 'population dynamics' and 'predator–prey relationships'. To start with, these were simple models, but with advances in scientific knowledge they have become more complex. Today the challenge is to try to incorporate into these models all the different aspects of fishing as a social and economic activity.

The management of fishing effort is divided into two complementary, and sometimes contradictory, areas: stock management, and management of the means of production. The science of stock management uses population dynamics and the biology of species to evaluate the current status of stocks being fished, and to then set optimum catch levels. Its reasoning is that the biomass of a fish stock varies according to four factors – the rate of reproduction, growth rate, natural mortality rate, and the catch rate (called 'rate of fishing mortality'). These factors have to be balanced and managed in order to guarantee optimum exploitation, and to ensure the sustainability of fish stocks.

If the harvesting rate of a stock is in balance with the natural rate of resource renewal, through recruitment of young fish and normal growth, the stock will continue to thrive. This ideal balance, however, is only theoretical. In practice, biological parameters fluctuate with environmental conditions, and the intensity of fishing effort varies unpredictably.

As a response, the new generation of fishery management models increasingly takes into account climatic and socio-economic data, in addition to biological data. For example, the study of fleet dynamics seeks to incorporate information about fleet structure, movements, strategy, and technical and economic characteristics. All these factors help to evaluate the optimum fishing effort needed as a function of the biological potential available. Increasingly pre- and post-harvest commercial activities are also taken into account.

Obviously, such a holistic approach, which tries to rationalize all these different aspects, complicates defining the fish stock system to be managed. The analysis is made particularly difficult by the multiplicity of interactions among the various elements.

In short, planning fisheries management is highly complex, but it is often tackled by over-simplification and with recourse to arbitration (which is often subjective). Both strategies are far from ideal.

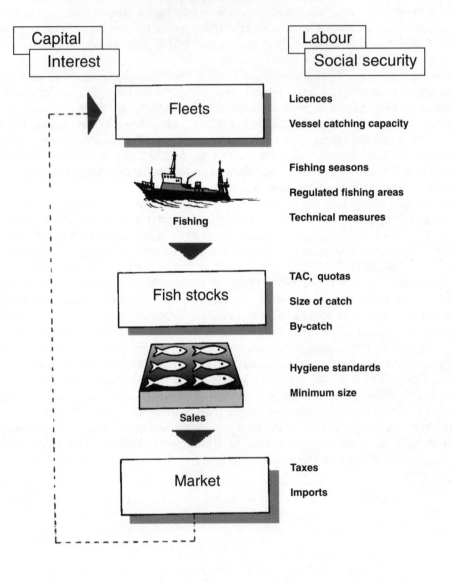

Regulatory measures operate at different levels

Capital
Interest

Labour
Social security

Fleets

Licences

Vessel catching capacity

Fishing seasons

Regulated fishing areas

Technical measures

Fishing

Fish stocks

TAC, quotas

Size of catch

By-catch

Hygiene standards

Minimum size

Sales

Market

Taxes

Imports

Source : Mustapha Ould El Kettab

© A Le Sann – CRISLA, 1995

Management objectives should be rationalized

In most countries the fishery is regulated by a 'management system' made up of a set of instruments and institutions whose main functions are to regulate fishing activities. Around the world, numerous systems have been tried and tested. These can be classified into two main types: direct systems and indirect systems. The direct systems limit access to fish stocks (through measures like licensing, fishing seasons, and closure of zones), restrict the technical efficiency of fishing equipment (through controls on vessel capacity and fishing gear), and regulate the catch (through Total Allowable Catch or TAC, quotas, minimum size of fish, and by-catch limits). Indirect systems function through socio-economic mechanisms like market interventions, taxation, and subsidies.

These different management systems are by no means mutually exclusive, but are often complementary. They are rarely universally applied, and must be applied and adapted to suit different situations. The effectiveness and acceptance of a management system in a given fishery will depend on how well it can be adapted to the biological, economic, social and institutional context of that particular fishery.

The objectives set for any management system will determine its content, but in general there will be three main purposes:

- To conserve resources: in this case, the management system strives to limit pressure on fish stocks by restricting fishing activity (called 'fishing effort').
- To help maintain the activity of those who fish for a living, and to sustain allied industries. Here, socio-economic regulation is required and success has to be evaluated in terms of distribution of income and social harmony.
- To increase profitability: in this case, regulation occurs indirectly, via market mechanisms (private acquisition of fishing rights, for example). Success is measured by the resulting financial flows.

Whatever the steps proposed, all development strategies ultimately arrive at the same conclusion: the need to rationalize the exploitation of fish stocks. But which rationale should be adopted? This is where things start to get complicated for fisheries management. Perspectives of rationality can differ drastically for an industrial ship-owner, a small fishing business, a consumer, or an ecologist. In such a context, drawing up a fisheries development policy and choosing methods are likely to require considerable compromise.

Towards participatory management

From management based on economic and administrative criteria

(1)

Fish stocks

Analysis

Biologists

Information

Economic policy market

Political considerations - government

Decisions

Decisions

Pressure

Fishworkers

Environmentalists

- -

(2)   ... towards community control

Environmentalists

Fishery

Analysis

Consultation

Scientists (biologists, economists, sociologists)

Fishworkers

Business partners

Government departments

Decision

© A Le Sann – CRISLA, 1995

Participatory management

In setting objectives (which are often too biological) and in their application (too depen-dent on bureaucracy and market forces), fisheries management regimes are often inap-propriate. When the biological dimension of fishing is considered in isolation, authorities may end up neglecting the basic issue at stake – it is not so much the fish stocks that need managing, as the ecosystem itself. This requires a much more complex approach. In addition, all too often, the sociological aspects are ignored (see *Crisis in the World's Fisheries: People, problems, and politics*, James R. McGoodwin, 1990).

Administrative decisions are often imposed and market forces are blind. In neither case are the main players in the fishing sector consulted, and this is bound to result in inefficient regulation.

However, numerous examples show that community management of fishing grounds is, in fact, possible. The success of this type of management depends upon two pre-requisites: the existence of organized communities and the delimitation of fishing zones. The best example of community management of fishing is undoubtedly that of Japan, where fishing co-operatives manage coastal waters and are responsible for allocating fishing zones and resolving disputes, while deep-sea fishing and fishing for migratory species involves state participation and control.

In the Philippines, in Panguil Bay, on the island of Mindanao, the fisheries development strategy depends upon the community management of 18 500 hectares, along a coastline of 116 km, involving 450 000 inhabitants. Since 1990, spectacular results have been obtained in replanting mangroves, monitoring fishing regulations and constructing artifi-cial reefs.

Management systems, however, are subject to constant change. The introduction of new fishing techniques can modify the fishing grounds, while diversifying the use of marine areas implies that other activities have to be managed as well.

All around the world, fishing communities are tending to disintegrate, in the face of modernization and depopulation, or with the appearance of new players on the scene. In Japan, the crisis in coastal fishing has led to the collapse of many professional fishing operations, while sport fishing has grown in popularity and is getting integrated into the sphere of fishing co-operatives.

Stages in the land-based production of Surimi

1 Delivery of whole fish

2 Gutting, removing
   heads, and skinning

3 Three washing
   and draining
   cycles

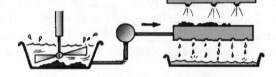

4 Disposal of residual waste
   (scales, skin and
   bones)

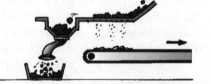

5 Addition of
   cryoprotective agents
   (sorbitol-saccharose
   and polyphosphates)

6 Freezing and storage   Overall yield : 30%

Make the best of fish as food

The full nutritional value of fish can best be realized by reducing waste and encouraging direct human consumption of fish. Transforming fish into animal feed as fishmeal is tremendously wasteful. But, since there is obviously a limit to the amount of fresh fish that can be consumed, other ways of preserving fish, such as canning or salting, have to be developed.

Many fish species can be canned, but low profitability is an obstacle. In Peru, many canneries find it more profitable to make fishmeal which is increasing in price, especially since rising aquaculture production provides more outlets for fishmeal (fishmeal being the main ingredient in feed used in intensive aquaculture of prawns and salmon, for example). In some cases, the quantity that needs to be processed exceeds the capacity of the canneries. In Chile, for instance, a single boat can catch 70 000 tonnes of fish per year.

Plainly, new systems are needed to handle the huge quantities of fish landed by South American fishermen. One possibility is the manufacture of surimi, a fish paste, which can be undertaken by small businesses as well as large factories.

The production of surimi, a traditional Japanese technique of preserving fish, became commercialized at the beginning of the twentieth century. Subsequently, in the 1950s and 1960s, a method of using frozen fish to make surimi was introduced. Today, Japan is still the leading manufacturer, accounting for 40 per cent of the 700 000 tonnes of surimi produced worldwide.

However, since taking over pollack fishing in Alaska, the United States has become a strong competitor. All the same production is often carried out through joint ventures with Japanese companies, which account for 20 per cent of world production. Trials are now under way to produce surimi with less popular species of fish, such as sardines which are fatty fish. Although many of these trials have ended in failure, there is a strong market demand.

Transforming fish into surimi certainly involves some wastage, but the overall yield of 25–30 per cent, coupled with the possibility of using part of the waste for fishmeal, means that these losses are still far below those that occur when fish is converted directly into fishmeal.

It should be stressed, however, that surimi is only one possibility among several for processing fish. Traditional methods of drying, smoking, and canning should also be encouraged.

Choose selective and appropriate technology

The crisis in South Indian traditional fisheries at the end of the 1970s

- Scarcity of timber to construct canoes and catamarans
- Coastal fish stocks exhausted
- Growth of industrial shrimp trawling

OPTIONS

Government

NGOs and artisanal fishworkers' organizations

Support for trawler construction, purse-seiners, and for shrimp exports

- Modernization of traditional craft (canoes and catamarans)
- Development of new boat designs
- Motorization, with outboard motors
- Both line and net fishing activities continue

CONSEQUENCES

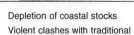

Depletion of coastal stocks

Violent clashes with traditional fishermen

Over-investment with government support

Development of large port areas

Extension of fishing zones

Increased productivity

New vessels at lower cost

Continued activity on the beaches

Problems associated with motorization and energy costs

Source: P Gillet

Choose environmentally sound and selective fishing techniques

However effective a particular fishing technique appears at first, it will always ultimately reveal some drawbacks. Techniques must be carefully evaluated; otherwise, the industry may find itself committed for several years to boosting fishing capacity in a way that may be disastrous.

Among the most crucial issues facing the industry are the cost of energy and the selectivity and efficiency of fishing gear. In terms of energy, both industrial and modernized artisanal fishing are extremely costly. It is estimated that about one litre of fuel is needed for every kilogram of fish landed. The industry is therefore very vulnerable to fluctuations in oil prices. In the modernized artisanal sector, petrol or kerosene-powered outboard motors are preferred, even though they are more expensive to run than inboard diesel motors which consume less fuel but are heavier and slower. New outboard diesel engines are becoming more popular.

The choice of fishing gear has far-reaching consequences. Electronics and motorization have made fishing gear so efficient as to put unprecedented pressure on fish stocks. The threat is particularly severe since dragged gear can never really be selective and catches unwanted species along with immature fish. Dragged gear can also inflict considerable damage to the sea bed and associated fish habitats. This is why some fishworkers' organizations have called for a total ban on trawling, at least in certain seas.

Obviously, the adoption of any new fishing techniques leads to a host of consequences. It is important that these be reflected upon and discussed within the fishing communities themselves. For Pierre Gillet, an engineer who specializes in the modernization of traditional fishing craft, a fishing technique is appropriate if it meets the following criteria:

- It results in increased productivity.
- It is accepted and used by fishermen.
- Its cost is accessible to the majority.
- It is ecologically sound, threatening neither the environment nor the fish stocks.
- It does not create new dependencies.

(See *Small is Difficult*, Pierre Gillet, IT Publications and CAT, 1985.)

In the end, however, the growth of fishworkers' incomes is related to higher productivity, at least as long as fish stocks allow continued exploitation of resources. Once the optimum catch level has been reached, incomes can only rise if the number of fishermen is reduced (by, for example, developing alternative occupations) or if the value of fish increases through better marketing or by regulating the market itself.

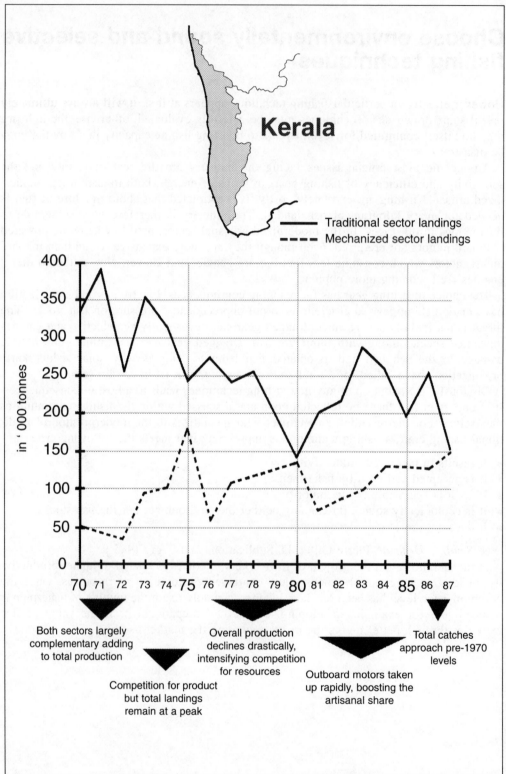

Kerala

Traditional sector landings
Mechanized sector landings

in ' 000 tonnes

400
350
300
250
200
150
100
50
0

70 71 72 73 74 75 76 77 78 79 80 81 82 83 84 85 86 87

Both sectors largely
complementary adding
to total production

Competition for product
but total landings
remain at a peak

Overall production
declines drastically,
intensifying competition
for resources

Outboard motors taken
up rapidly, boosting the
artisanal share

Total catches
approach pre-1970
levels

© A Le Sann – CRISLA, 1997

Kerala bans trawling

Kerala, India's premier marine fish-producing state, has been going through a deep crisis in its fisheries. It is a crisis which has arisen through the application of a particular approach to development pursued by the Government in the 1960s. The upshot of this was the creation of a modern commercial fishery sector, using trawling technology introduced from Norway (where, paradoxically enough, it had been banned in coastal waters) and targeting an export market for prawns.

While undoubtedly significant benefits have accrued to the Indian economy through the generation of foreign exchange, it is questionable how equitably these benefits have been distributed. The degree to which overfishing has occurred also raises the question of how sustainable the fishery can now be in the long term, and how the thousands of fishery-dependent people will earn their livelihoods, should the fishery collapse.

In the late 1970s, the violent protests against the trawlers became more organized through the establishment of artisanal fishworkers' unions. In 1978, the fishermen leaders from the States of Goa, Kerala and Tamil Nadu came together to discuss the need for collective action on a national scale. This resulted in the constitution of the National Fishworkers' Forum (NFF).

In Kerala, in the early 1980s, the Kerala Independent Fishworkers' Federation began to organize large-scale demonstrations, and to press the government to adopt and implement the Kerala Marine Fishing Regulation Act. This was passed in 1980, and was designed to protect the artisanal fishery from the encroachment of mechanized trawlers and purse-seiners. The Act contained two principal measures of interest to the artisanal sector:

- The restriction of mechanized trawling to beyond a distance of about 10 km (i.e. the reservation of an exclusive coastal fishing zone for the artisanal fishery).
- The imposition of a ban on trawling during the 'monsoon' months of June to August, which was believed to be the spawning season for many fish species valuable to the artisanal sector.

While some success had been achieved in persuading the State Government to adopt this Act, there was clearly a lack of political will to implement it. It was only in 1988, in response to extensive agitation by the fishworkers' unions, that the Government instituted a partial ban, which turned out to be ineffective in preventing trawlers from putting out to sea. In 1989, the Government implemented a complete ban for the three monsoon months of June, July and August.

The combination of this ban with particularly favourable environmental conditions resulted in very large pelagic fish landings in October 1989 (two months after the ban had been lifted). The introduction of 'mini purse seines' had also increased the ability of motorized boats to harvest large proportions of pelagic shoals.

In 1988 and 1989, fish harvests broke all records, with around 640 000 tonnes being landed in 1989: 240 000 tonnes above the estimated maximum sustainable yield.

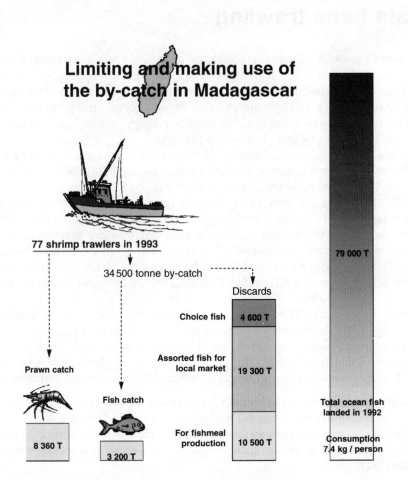

Limiting and making use of the by-catch in Madagascar

77 shrimp trawlers in 1993

34 500 tonne by-catch

Discards

Choice fish   4 600 T

Prawn catch

Assorted fish for local market   19 300 T

8 360 T

Fish catch

For fishmeal production   10 500 T

3 200 T

79 000 T

Total ocean fish landed in 1992

Consumption 7.4 kg / person

Example: One artisanal 7-metre collector vessel
(11 tonnes of fish sold in two months)...

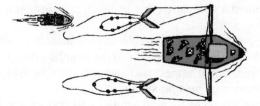

... provides work for 120 people
(mostly women)

Limitations
... causing discards

- Low price of fish compared to shrimps
- Storage problems
- Lack of land-based infrastructure and distribution channels

© A Le Sann – CRISLA, 1995

Limit by-catches

The problems associated with fish by-catches are becoming better known. People are moved by stories of dolphins killed by the seiners in the Eastern Pacific or by the drift-nets of French albacore tuna fishing vessels, and the plight of turtles in tropical waters being caught by prawn trawlers.

In Alaskan pollack fisheries, the rejected by-catch sometimes constitutes as much as 80 per cent of the total haul. In the South Pacific, during the 1988–89 fishing season, large drift-nets were estimated to have captured 23 000 whales. Each year, Japanese long-liners are responsible for the deaths of 44 000 birds (albatrosses and petrels) in the South Pacific ocean. Even though these examples of by-catch may relate to endangered species, there are fundamental issues which are far more significant – wastage of food, and the disruption of the ecological balance of the marine environment.

In this context, perhaps the most serious threat of all is the practice of trawling. Dragged gear can never be truly selective, even if regulating the size or shape of the mesh used in fishing nets can, to some degree, determine the size or type of fish caught. Trials are under way to improve the selectivity of trawls (for example, by using turtle excluder devices), but every net always catches some fish that are of no possible interest to the fisherman – unmarketable species, fish that are too small, or an assortment of low-value shellfish.

Trawling for prawns or shrimps poses a particularly severe problem since the mesh size of the net is very small. Numerous living organisms from the sea bed are captured along with the prawns, which at times make up as little as 10 per cent of the total catch. More often than not, juvenile fish are caught and killed immediately. This breaks the reproductive cycle of nutritionally important species and deprives coastal and neighbouring populations of food. Estimates of losses from this type of fishing range from 10 to 20 millions tonnes. Recently, the FAO set the figure even higher, at 27 million tonnes.

No wonder, then, that Indian artisanal fishworkers have demanded a total ban on trawling. Since 1982, a trawling ban has been in force throughout Western Indonesia. In North Yemen, at the end of the 1970s, coastal fishworkers successfully fought for a ban on trawling (see *L'Homme et les ressources halieutiques*, Jean-Paul Troadec, IFREMER, 1989).

Many experts argue that by-catch should be landed and used in the local market. Such landings can, however, have a negative impact on prices, and on the income of artisanal fishers. For example, in Madagascar, prawn trawlers hand over some of their surplus fish to artisanal fishermen, and in other countries by-catch is sold for the manufacture of fishmeal. In Guinea Bissau the landings of by-catch by foreign trawlers has a negative impact on the incomes of local fishermen, as it floods the market with low-value fish.

Concerted action is needed to devise and implement solutions capable of solving the increasing problem of wastage and ecological damage caused by non-selective fishing techniques.

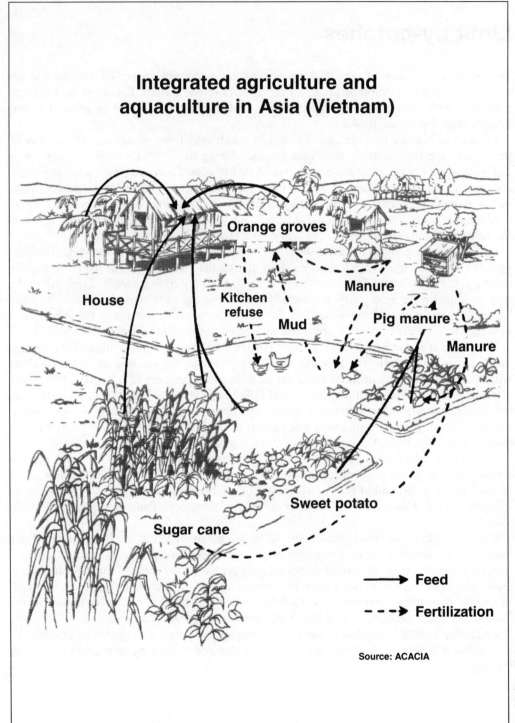

Integrated agriculture and aquaculture in Asia (Vietnam)

House

Orange groves

Kitchen refuse

Manure

Mud

Pig manure

Manure

Sweet potato

Sugar cane

⟶ Feed

- - -▶ Fertilization

Source: ACACIA

Promote extensive aquaculture

Nobody knows for sure the precise origin of aquaculture, but it is likely that it has existed for several thousands of years. In a work dating around 475 BC, Fan Li describes Chinese techniques of integrated aquaculture. These involved the extensive rearing of a variety of species of carp in ponds, feeding them on agricultural by-products such as pig or poultry excrement or vegetable refuse. Today this practice is still the basis for much of Asian aquaculture.

Currently, aquaculture in China (excluding algae production) contributes more than seven million tonnes per annum or nearly half the worldwide production of aquatic animals. More than five species of carp are raised together in order to optimize the use of ponds and available feed (vegetable refuse, pig litter and poultry droppings). Despite the use of such rudimentary technology, yields comparable to those from intensive aquaculture are sometimes obtained. Chinese researchers are currently working to improve the overall productivity, which can vary widely, from 1.5 tonnes to 12 tonnes of fish per hectare per year.

Other examples of this kind of traditional aquaculture are algae culture in Japan, and oyster and mussel farming in Europe. Like carp farming in China, these activities blend with the rural environment and makes the best use of open waters.

The other attractive feature of this so-called 'extensive aquaculture' is that it uses unsophisticated techniques that are accessible to all farmers. Extensive aquaculture is the most widespread form of aquaculture and accounts for nearly 90 per cent of the world's production. It is practised in open areas like lakes, estuaries or coastal bays, where nutrients are supplied naturally by the local environment. It supports numerous families without harming the environment. Over the centuries, it has shown itself not only commercially viable but also capable of producing substantial quantities of inexpensive animal protein.

Nevertheless, it must be noted that China, too, has lately succumbed to the attraction of quick profits from intensive prawn aquaculture. So have many other Asian countries. China has rapidly gone on to become the world's leading producer, but, since 1993, signs have appeared of ecological disruption of the marine environment.

Both Taiwan and China, two of the former leading shrimp-farming nations, have experienced 'environmental backlash' on a nationwide scale. Taiwanese shrimp production slumped from 100 000 tonnes in 1987 to only 20 000 tonnes in 1989 and China's 1992 harvest was down 60 per cent on the previous year. Both countries' shrimp-farming industries have been slow to recover. In each case the cause was the same: the widespread and uncontrollable outbreak of disease, a result of poor water quality and increasingly toxic ponds.

France
The market for scallops, 1991–92

Withdrawal price
(F/kg)

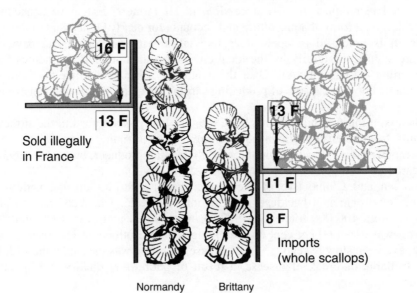

16 F

13 F

Sold illegally
in France

13 F

11 F

8 F

Imports
(whole scallops)

Normandy   Brittany

8 000 T   **50 000 T**

Source : *France Eco Péche.* February 1992

Regulate the markets

The history of marine fishing has been marked by crises caused by either the absence or overabundance of fish stocks. By nature, fishing is a see-saw activity. This trait makes it a source of great hardship for fishermen. In many areas the heavy investment required in fishing boats or gear has made fishworkers very dependent on boat-owning companies, canning factories or wholesale fishmongers for employment opportunities.

During periods of crisis, fishermen's attempts to control prices have been hindered by technical or ecological factors and by the mobility of capital. Governments are better placed. In the Cape Verde Islands, for instance, when prices fall below a fixed minimum price, the government is committed to buying up all the surplus. This concerns mostly tuna, for which the government owns warehousing and processing facilities.

In the 1970s, EU producers' organizations were able to set up a system involving state intervention to maintain market prices. When prices fell below floor level (calculated as an average of market prices for the preceding three years), fishermen belonging to a producers' organization would withhold a proportion of their produce from the market in order to push prices up. They would also receive compensation, financed by their own subscriptions and by the EU. Produce withdrawn from the market was preserved by salting, cooking or freezing. Efforts were made to avoid the conversion of fish into fishmeal. The producers' organization similarly drew up a strategy to limit catches when supply persistently exceeded demand.

Apart from a few hitches, this system functioned well for several years, until borders opened up and globalization led to the total deregulation of the world's marketplaces. Once borders no longer afforded protection, price variations in Europe intensified. How, for example, could a floor price of FF16 per kilogram of scallops be maintained when massive imports of the same product (up to five times the national production levels) sell for half the price? The crisis also eroded discipline among members and especially among non-members who sell at any price, and over and above permitted quantities, in order to maintain their incomes.

In the absence of border controls, market mechanisms are ineffective in protecting incomes. Doubtless, it will become necessary to protect incomes by controlling the levels of investment, by introducing fishing methods that do not destroy the environment and by improving working conditions. In the end, one of the only possible means for achieving this is an increasingly strong organization of professional fishworkers worldwide.

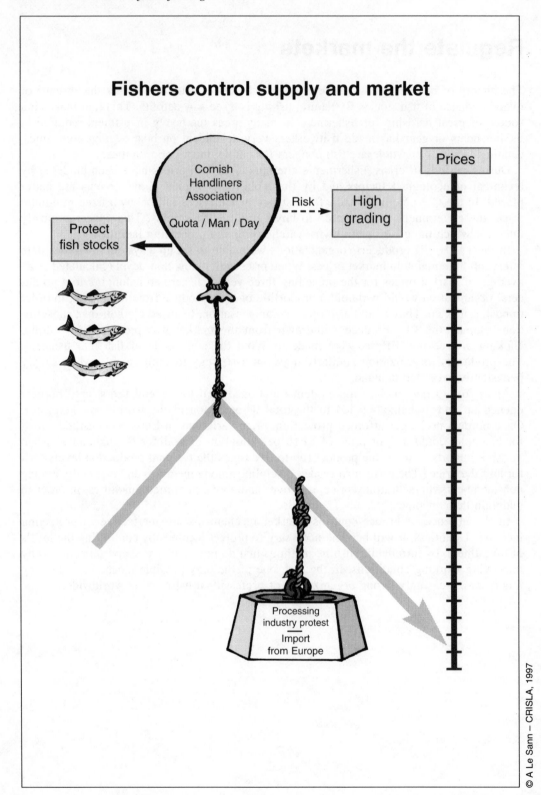

Fishers control supply and market

Cornish
Handliners
Association
———
Quota / Man / Day

Risk

High
grading

Protect
fish stocks

Prices

Processing
industry protest
———
Import
from Europe

How free and fair is the free market?

Most fishworkers agree: fishing is a gamble. It is a game of chance played against the weather, the chance of a good catch, and the chance of a good market price. With the advent of safer boats and improved fish-locating technology, in many parts of the world the market has become the key factor in determining whether fishworkers make a profit or a loss. The market is also one of the key factors driving the demand for fish, and puts pressure indirectly on fish stocks.

There are many merchants and dealers who 'play the market' by restricting supply, thereby increasing effective demand and price. This is regarded as fair game. Such restrictive practices have also been attempted by fishworkers as supply-side conservation measures which also serve to raise the prices received. However, these attempts by fishworkers to restrict supply to improve their incomes and to conserve fish stocks are often met with hostility by the processing and marketing sectors.

In Senegal, in the community of Kayar, the local fishworkers' organization controls the quantity of fish landed by its members. They have recognized that it is better value to sell one box of 'pageot' (sea bream) at 4000 CFA francs than three boxes at 1000 CFA francs. Fish stocks are better protected, and the fishermen earn a better living.

In 1993/94 in Cornwall, UK, a small group of fishermen belonging to the Cornish Handliners' Association attempted to control the market by limiting supply. They implemented a self-imposed quota, which restricted the size of landings to 25 stone (about 160 kg) per person per day. For a short time this had a beneficial effect on prices, but ran up against problems with the bulk/industrial market. The prices went up until the merchants began to bring in mackerel from outside. The Association was criticized by the processing industry for restricting supplies and for inflating prices above profitable levels.

These attempts to limit market supply and thus increase earnings were frustrated by imports of fish from Europe. In Scotland, the Scottish Restrictive Practices Court declared illegal the practice of restricting fishing for the purpose of raising fish prices. In the USA, the Massachusetts Supreme Court found the limitation of catches by the New England fishing industry illegal, due to the intended effect on fish prices.

Supply-side control is the practice of many large fish processing companies to hold back stocks of frozen fish when prices are low, and artificially control prices on the market by releasing supplies of fish gradually.

As a conservation measure, supply-side controls should be encouraged. However, in some instances, such controls may only serve to encourage 'high grading', causing the wastage of much marketable fish with associated harmful effects on fish stocks. Under such circumstances they should clearly be discouraged.

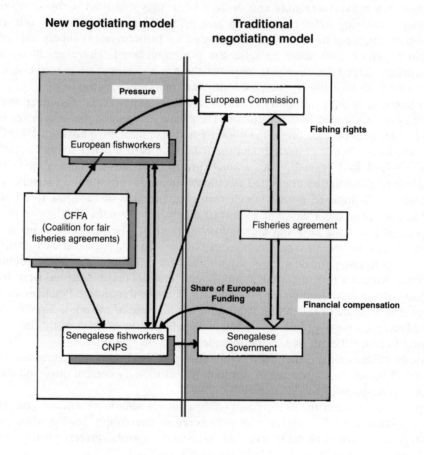

Re-thinking fisheries agreements

European Union – Senegal

New negotiating model

Traditional negotiating model

Pressure

European Commission

European fishworkers

Fishing rights

CFFA
(Coalition for fair
fisheries agreements)

Fisheries agreement

**Share of European
Funding**

Financial compensation

Senegalese fishworkers
CNPS

Senegalese
Government

Classical negotiation

Since 1989

© A Le Sann – CRISLA, 1995

Review fisheries agreements

Almost everyone concerned with international fisheries agreements now wants them revised – and fast. The EU considers the compensatory payments for fishing rights they access through fishery agreements too costly, especially since these rights are not always used, due to the depletion of stocks. Again because of stock depletion, the ACP countries realize that they are caught in an impasse. When it comes to negotiation, they no longer have sufficient stocks to bargain with.

Following independence, Namibia refused to sign a fisheries agreement with the EU which would not have guaranteed any real development for its own fishing industry. Instead, it preferred to encourage joint ventures for fish processing on Namibian territory so as to extract maximum value added on home ground itself. Island nations in the South Pacific have established the Forum Fisheries Agency (FFA) to negotiate on their behalf with nations such as the United States, which want access to the fish stocks in their EEZs.

Artisanal fishworkers are well aware of the negative effects of fisheries agreements. They have protested their exclusion from the negotiating process and the absence of financial returns for local fishing and processing industries. In Senegal, fishworkers belonging to the CNPS have struggled to make their voices heard in the negotiations between their country and Europe. In 1994 they successfully negotiated for about 1 per cent of the compensation payment from the EU fisheries to be invested in the artisanal sector. This amounted to some 200 000 ECU (or 130 million CFA Francs). This initial victory, modest as it is, should inspire fishworkers in other ACP countries (see *Gaal-Gui*, January 1995).

Several European NGOs have formed the Coalition for Fair Fisheries Agreements (CFFA). CFFA is working for fundamental change in the EC's policy and practice on fisheries agreements with countries in the South (ACP States and others). Its particular concerns are the sustainable use of fish resources for the benefit of fishing communities who depend on them for their livelihoods and food security, and the conservation of global fish stocks for future generations.

Objectives for a code of conduct for responsible fishing

Protect coastline

Prevent over-fishing

Use selective fishing gear

Resolve disputes peacefully

Protect fishworkers' rights and working conditions

... at sea

... on land

Conserve, nurture and develop bio-aquatic resources and aquatic ecosystems

Precautionary approach

Bring fishworkers and policymakers together

Source : FAO

© A Le Sann – CRISLA, 1995

Implement a code of conduct for responsible fisheries

To promote the sustainability of fisheries, the Food and Agriculture Organization (FAO) has developed a Code of Conduct for Responsible Fisheries. This sets out to harmonize the environmental, social and economic aspects of the use of fisheries resources, and was approved by the FAO Conference in 1995. Member States (including all EU member states) of the FAO are therefore bound by its provisions. The Code is directed to all those involved in fisheries and it provides a comprehensive framework for establishing coherence between potentially conflicting interests and policies.

Given the deepening crisis in global fisheries prevalent at the beginning of the 1990s, the Government of Mexico and the FAO took the initiative to organize a 'Conference on Responsible Fisheries' in Mexico. This gave rise to the Declaration of Cancun in May 1992, which defines responsible fisheries as, inter alia:

. . . the sustainable utilization of fisheries resources in harmony with the environment, the use of capture and aquaculture practices which are not harmful to ecosystems, resources, or their quality; the incorporation of added value to such products through transformation processes meeting the required sanitary standards, the conduct of commercial practices so as to provide consumers access to good quality products.

The Code also promotes the application of the precautionary approach to fisheries management, the integration of fisheries into coastal area management, the use of selective and environmentally safe fishing gear, and responsible aquaculture.

The concept of responsibility and sustainable development was also very much part of the UNCED process. Chapter 17 of Agenda 21 of UNCED (which deals with oceans and coastal areas – the so-called 'Oceans Chapter') agrees that further measures are required to ensure the effective implementation of UNCLOS. While UNCLOS confers ownership and fishing rights to States, UNCED's Rio Declaration points out that the right to fish is conditional and accompanied by the duty to manage and conserve resources for present and future generations.

Despite the limitations of voluntary regulation, this Code marks a real step forward, especially since the FAO has made efforts to bring together fishworkers' organizations, environmental protection groups and NGOs to assist its development, and implementation.

The Code also recognizes the important contribution of artisanal and small-scale fisheries to employment, income and food security, and calls upon states to protect their rights to resource access, to decent working conditions, and to livelihood security.

In criticism, though, it must be said that the Code is profoundly liberal in character, and concedes to the principles of the World Trade Organization, which favour the flow of seafood from South to North.

Glossary

ACP states: African, Pacific and Caribbean states, party to the Lomé Convention (qv).

Active fishing gears: Active fishing gears are those which actively come into contact with the fish; for example, gears like trawl nets and purse seines, which are towed and manoeuvred by the boat. *See* Passive fishing gears.

Aquaculture: Aquatic animal and plant production, or the farming or culture of seaweeds, shellfish and molluscs as well as fish.

Artificial reef: A human structure placed in the sea, and fixed on the sea bed, to act as an 'artificial reef'. At best artificial reefs will enhance natural fisheries production by providing a new habitat, but will almost certainly attract fish from a much wider area making them easier to catch.

Artisanal fishing: Subsistence, traditional or small-scale fishing. Often based around family units or communities, with the men engaged in fish catching, and the women in processing, transport and marketing. Generally carried out in small, open boats (such as canoes and similar craft), which may be motorized with simple engines (like outboard motors), using simple nets and lines. Artisanal fisheries provide the mainstay of fishery production in most countries of the South, contributing significantly to local food security, employment and income.

Bathometry: The measurement of ocean depth.

Benthic: Bottom-dwelling and feeding fish (and other aquatic organisms) such as sole, crayfish, and sea urchins.

Biomass: In fisheries, the quantity (by weight) of a given fish population or other biological population. Used, for example, to define the size of a fish population or the quantity of food available to it. Literally the total mass of living matter (animal or vegetal) contained in an ecosystem.

Blue Europe: A term given to the European fisheries instruments (i.e. policies, regulations, etc.) and institutions, and relating to the Common Fisheries Policy of the European Union.

Brackish water: Saline water resulting from the mix of fresh water and sea water, generally with salt concentrations below pure sea water (33 parts per thousand).

Brush park: Shallow water (often lagoon) area planted with palm leaves and other structures which serve as fish habitats. Function both to aggregate fish and to enhance natural production.

By-catch: The part of the fish catch which is discarded because it contains either fish of low economic value, or fish which are not allowed to be caught (e.g. under-size, over-quota or otherwise protected species – as when dolphins are caught along with tuna, or turtles are caught by shrimp trawls).

Capture fisheries: Fishing as a hunting activity, as opposed to a harvesting activity like aquaculture or mariculture.

Catchment area: Area drained by a river system – i.e. which catches the run-off from the land and feeds it into the river systems. Lakes, streams, rivers and estuaries all have catchment areas (*see* Watershed).

CCFD: *Comité Catholique contre la Faim et pour le Développement* (4 rue Jean-Lantier, 75001 Paris) – the French NGO, Catholic Committee against Hunger and for Development.

CFA franc: Unit of currency used in francophone West Africa, in the CFA zone. This comprises 12 West African countries, including Senegal, Benin, Burkina Faso, Congo, Ivory Coast, Cameroon, Gabon, Mali, Niger and Togo.

CFP: the Common Fisheries Policy of the European Union for managing and conserving fish stocks in its own waters. It establishes common rules for all member nations, and covers all aspects of the fishing industry from the sea to the consumer. The CFP also deals with fishery agreements with other coastal nations.

CNPS: Collectif National des Pêcheurs artisanaux Sénégalais – the National Collective of Senegalese Artisanal Fishermen, an independent organization of artisanal fishermen founded in 1987, which now has women members too.

Continental shelf: The sub-sea area surrounding the land masses, which extends from the coastal shallows to depths of between 150 and 250 metres. The end of the continental shelf is marked by a sharp increase in gradient.

Coral reef: Rocky formations produced by coral settlement and growth.

CRISLA: *Centre de Réflexion, d'Information et de Solidarité avec les peuples d'Afrique, d'Asie et d'Amérique Latine* – the Centre for Reflection, Information and Solidarity with the People of Africa, Asia and Latin America, based at 1 Avenue de la Marne, 56100 Lorient, France.

CTA: *Centre Technique de coopération Agricole et rurale* (the Technical Centre for Agriculture and Rural Co-operation), under EU management.

Distant water fishing: Where one nation's fishing fleet fishes outside its own EEZ (qv), either in the EEZ of another or on the high seas.

Demersal: Fish found on or near the sea bed, such as hake, cod, or pollack, without being totally dependent on bottom-feeding (*see* Benthic and Pelagic).

Drift-net: A net suspended vertically in the sea by means of floats along the top edge and weights along the bottom edge. Drift-nets can exceed 50 km in length.

Echo sounder: Also referred to as 'sonar' or 'fish finder', an instrument used for locating fish by acoustic means.

ECU: European currency unit, used for administrative purposes in the European Union – a standard which is used to calculate EU financial transactions.

EEC/European Union/EU: Established in 1957 by the treaty of Rome, the European Economic Community (the EEC or Common Market) subsequently evolved first into the European Community and finally into the European Union through the Maastricht Treaty (Treaty on European Union) of 1991. In 1997 the EU comprised 15 member nations.

EEZ: Exclusive Economic Zone – national and (in the case of the EU) regional boundaries extending 200 miles to sea, where the coastal state has jurisdiction over all marine resources (including exclusive rights and responsibilities for their exploration, exploitation and management). Internationally recognized through the United Nations Convention on the Law of the Sea (UNCLOS, qv).

FAD: Fish Aggregating Device – often a free-floating raft or other structure designed to attract fish.

FAO: The Food and Agriculture Organization, a specialized agency of the United Nations.

Filleting: The removal of bones from a fish to produce fillets.

Fin fish: Literally fish with fins, but used to describe all species of fish with back bones (*see* Shellfish).

Fingerlings: Juvenile fish of the required size (literally finger size) for stocking ponds or other water areas.

Fisheries agreement: A formal agreement signed between states whereby the vessels of one state are allowed to fish in the EEZ (qv) of another, in exchange for financial compensation, market access, etc. For example, the European Union spends some 30–40 per cent of its total fisheries budget on securing access for its distant water fleet.

Fishery: Fish stocks exploited by a fleet in a given geographical area.

Fishing effort: A measure of the intensity of fishing, usually defined by the number, size (tonnage), and power (horse power) of boats, combined with the number of days spent fishing.

Fishing gears: Nets, lines, hooks, etc. used for the capture and extraction of fish.

Fishmeal: An important industrial product derived from processing and drying fish. Used mainly for animal feeds.

Fish stock: Fish population (or part of one) located in a defined geographical area, not interacting with neighbouring fish stocks of the same species. The term is not a biological concept, but a theoretical unit used in fisheries management.

Fishworker: Any man, woman or child engaged in the fishing industry – whether as crew member, small fisher, processing worker or petty trader. Generally a term used to describe the artisanal sector.

Food chain: The sum total of living matter linked together through their feeding habits. For example, phytoplankton (primary producer) is eaten by zooplankton (a consumer) which is, in turn, eaten by sand eels, which are then eaten by herring, which are then caught by cormorants or by man. Food chains are usually highly complex pyramid-shaped structures, with numerous species situated at each level.

Food security: Recently defined as 'access by all people at all times to enough food for an active, healthy life', highlighting the importance of access. However, food security depends not only on availability of food, but also on people having the necessary purchasing power (or means of exchange) to acquire food, and social relationships which allow them access to it within the household.

GATT: General Agreement on Tariffs and Trade, which came into force on 1 January 1948. Initiated by eight countries, the purpose of GATT was to provide a secure and predictable international trading environment to encourage investment, job creation and so on. GATT was concerned primarily with stimulating international trade by reducing barriers such as quotas and tariffs (*see* Uruguay Round and WTO).

GESAMP: Group of Experts on the Scientific Aspects of Marine Pollution, a United Nations committee.

GRET: *Groupe de Recherche et d'Echanges Technologique*, an independent association which carries out research into projects and strategies for development.

Hatchery: That part of a fish farm or aquaculture unit which produces and hatches fish spawn (eggs), often through controlled breeding (involving selection of brood stock and induced spawning through injection of hormones). A hatchery produces 'hatchlings', larvae and young fish for on-growing in aquaculture production.

High-seas fishing: Fishing outside EEZs (qv) in international waters.

ICSF: International NGO – International Collective in Support of Fishworkers: 65 rue Gréty, B-1000, Brussels, Belgium and 27 College Road, Madras, India.

Industrial fishing: Fishing aimed at supplying the raw material for the fishmeal industry, which turns it into animal feed for pigs or poultry, for example, or extracts fish oil and other by-products from it. Often also used to describe capital-intensive, modern, mechanized, technically advanced fishing operations, carried out in purpose-built boats (trawlers, purse-seiners, drift-netters etc.).

Joint venture: A contractual relationship between commercial enterprises (ship owners, fish processors, etc.) from one nation and those in another (third country), where a joint business is established for the purpose of jointly exploiting and/or processing the third country's fishery resources.

Juveniles: Immature fish.

Lomé Convention: A comprehensive trade and development agreement between the European Union and 69 countries in the South which are generally referred to as the African, Caribbean and Pacific or ACP states (qv).

Long-line: A system of fishing where long lines of (generally baited) hooks are used to catch certain fish species. Often carried out from a purpose-built ship or long-liner.

MSY: Maximum Sustainable Yield, a fishery management concept, where for a given fish population there is a maximum level of exploitation, above which the 'yield' – economic (i.e. profit) and biological – declines.

Nautical mile (or sea mile): 1852 metres (slightly longer than an ordinary mile).

NGOs: Non-governmental organizations are associations, groups or collectives set up with a variety of functions. Increasingly they act to influence development policy-making at both national and international levels. NGOs have been officially recognized for several years now by international organizations such as the UN as being important interest groups and stake holders in international negotiations in their own right.

The North: The industrialized or so-called developed countries. The term was coined by the Brandt Commission Report (North-South), which identified that most of the industrial production, consumption and wealth was in the Northern hemisphere.

Nursery: Often in coastal areas close to shore, an area where young fish congregate and feed until they reach adult size and are recruited to the fishery.

OAU: Organization of African Unity.

Over-capitalization: Over-investment in fishing capital (boats, engines and gears) where low returns per unit investment make the fishery enterprise non-profitable. A symptom of over-capitalization is significant government subsidy to the fishing industry.

Overfishing: Where the level of fishing depletes resources at a faster rate than they can grow (growth overfishing), reproduce or be recruited to the fishery (recruitment over-fishing).

Passive fishing gears: Fishing gears which catch fish passively; for example, hand-lines, long-lines and gill-nets.

PCBs: Polychlorinated biphenyl, a toxic chemical waste from processing industry.

Pelagic: Fish that swim at the surface or in mid-water without any apparent dependence upon the sea bed; for example, sardines, anchovies and herring.

Phytoplankton: Microscopic aquatic (marine and freshwater) plant life.

Pirogues: Traditional fishing canoe used in Senegal and other West African countries. Often used as a general word to describe small fishing canoes used in artisanal fisheries.

Precautionary approach: A new approach to fisheries management. It requires that fishing activities be conducted in a manner which gives a high level of certainty that the risk of irreversible ecological damage is negligible.

Primary productivity: The mass of organic matter generated in an ecosystem by photo-synthesis and related processes (e.g. grass and phytoplankton production).

Purse seines: *See* Seine-nets.

Quota management: Management system for fisheries, which establishes quotas for particular stocks or species. These are allocated in various ways to fishing companies, producer organizations, or individual fishworkers. The way in which quotas are set and allocated has a significant bearing on resource management and conservation of stocks.

Recruitment: The natural increase in the size of a fish stock through the maturation and addition of young adult fish.

Seine-nets: Nets which catch fish by surrounding them. Include beach seines used by artisanal fishermen, and purse seines used in industrial and other large-scale fisheries for tuna, sardines, anchovy etc.

Seiner: A boat which catches fish by surrounding fish shoals with net.

Selectivity: The capacity of fishing gear to select fish of the desired size and species.

Shellfish: Literally fish with shells, including molluscs (e.g. squids, bivalves and snail-like species) and crustacea (e.g. lobster, crabs and prawns).

The South: The less-developed countries. A term coined by the Brandt Commission (North–South), which concluded that most of the indebted, poverty-stricken and economically disadvantaged countries are in the Southern hemisphere.

Spawning grounds: An area where fish eggs are deposited and fertilized.

Straddling stocks: Fish stocks whose range occurs over the boundaries of two or more EEZs, or between the EEZ of one country and international waters; those fish stocks whose range 'straddles' international boundaries.

Surimi: A food made from fish paste.

TAC: Total Allowable Catch – the quantity or quota of a given fish population (or populations) allowed to be caught, generally fixed annually.

Territorial waters: The sea area extending 12 miles from the shore, over which coastal states have sovereignty.

Third countries: In the case of fisheries, countries which allow other countries access to fish stocks in their EEZs through fisheries agreements – not to be confused with 'Third World'.

Third World: A rather out-of-date concept applied to less developed countries, where the industrialized countries or North were considered to comprise the First World, the Soviet Bloc the Second World, and all other countries the Third World.

Trawler/Trawl: A system of fishing where a bag-shaped net is dragged along the sea bed (demersal or bottom trawling) or in mid water (pelagic trawl). It may be towed by a single trawler, or by two boats (pair trawling). Often a highly destructive form of fishing which has a high rate of by-catch.

UNCED: United Nations Conference on Environment and Development, held in Rio de Janeiro in 1992. Produced the 'Rio Declaration', Agenda 21 and the Convention on Biological Diversity.

UNCLOS: United Nations Convention on the Law of the Sea. Adopted by the United Nations in 1982, UNCLOS only came into force in November 1994. UNCLOS has established as international law the concept of marine property rights, where it is recognized that national territorial waters extend to 12 nautical miles, whilst coastal states have jurisdiction over marine resources within 200 mile EEZs.

Upwelling: Cold waters, often nutrient-rich, rise from close to the ocean floor to the surface, generally where the cold waters meet the edge of the continental shelf (qv).

Uruguay Round: Between 1948 and 1979, seven 'rounds' of the GATT (qv) were held to try to liberalize international trade. The final, eighth round – the Uruguay Round – of the GATT was initiated in 1968 by 100 participant states. It covered 14 areas relating to trade and was concluded in December 1993. *See* WTO.

Watershed: Often used synonymously with catchment area (qv), but usually defines the boundary of a catchment area. The line separating the waters flowing into different rivers or river basins – often a narrow elevated tract of ground between two drainage areas.

WTO: The World Trade Organization is an independent organization established in 1995 to provide the institutional framework for the implementation of the multilateral trade agreements negotiated in the Uruguay Round (qv; *see* GATT).

Bibliography

Abramovitz, J.N. 1996. *Imperiled Waters, Impoverished Future: The decline of freshwater eco-systems*. Worldwatch Paper 128, March 1996, USA.

Bundell, K. and Maybin, E. 1996. *After the Prawn Rush*. Christian Aid, UK.

CFFA and CREDETIP. 1995. *Fishing for a Future*. CFFA, Brussels.

Clucas, I.J. and Ward, A.R. 1996. *Post-harvest Fisheries Development: A guide to handling, preservation, processing and quality*. NRI, UK.

FAO. 1993. *Marine Fisheries and the Law of the Sea: A decade of change*. Fisheries Circular No. 853, Rome.

FAO. 1995. *Review of the State of World Fishery Resources: Aquaculture*. FAO Fisheries Circular No. 886, Rome.

FAO. 1997. *The State of World Fisheries and Aquaculture 1996*, Rome.

Goldschmidt, J. 1996. *Darwin's Dreampond: Drama in Lake Victoria*. MIT Press, London, UK.

Fernandez J. 1994. *Artificial Fish Habitats – A Community Programme for Biodiversity Conservation*. Programme for Community Organisation, Kerala, India.

Finlayson, A.C. 1994. *Fishing for Truth*. Institute of Social and Economic Research Publications, Newfoundland, Canada.

Holden, M. 1994. *The Common Fisheries Policy*. Fishing News Books, UK.

Intermediate Technology, 1996. *Fisherfolk Safeguarding Aquatic Diversity Through Their Fishing Techniques*, ITDG, Rugby, UK.

IUCN. 1991. *Caring for the earth – a strategy for sustainable living*. Earthscan, London.

Kurien, J. 1996. *Towards a New Agenda for Sustainable Fisheries Development*. South Indian Federation of Fishermen Societies, Kerala, India.

Lewis, D.J., Wood, G.D., and Gregory, R. 1996. *Trading the Silver Seed*. IT Publications, London.

Maclean, R.H. and Jones, R.W. 1995. *Aquatic Biodiversity Conservation: A review of current issues and efforts*. Strategy for International Fisheries Research, Canada.

Madeley, J. 1996. *Trade and the Poor*. IT Publications, London.

Martinez, A. and Tudela, S. 1995. *Fish, Fleets and Markets: The effects of EU fishery policies on the South*. Coordinadora de ONGD, Madrid (c/ de la Reina, 17–3°, 28004 Madrid, Spain).

Mathew, S. 1990. *Fishing Legislation and Gear Conflicts in Asian Countries*. SAMUDRA Monograph, ICSF, Madras, India.

McGoodwin, J.R. 1990. *Crisis in the World's Fisheries: People, problems and policies*. Stanford Univ. Press, USA.

National Academy Press. 1994. *Improving the Management of US Marine Fisheries*. Committee on Fisheries, National Research Council, Washington DC, USA.

Norse, E. (ed.) 1993. *Marine Biological Diversity: A strategy for building conservation into decision-making*. Island Press, USA.

OECD: *Review of Fisheries in OECD Member Countries*. OECD Paris 1994.

Pomeroy, R.S. (ed.) 1994. *Community Management and Common Property of Coastal Fisheries in Asia and the Pacific: Concepts, methods and experiences*. ICLARM, Philippines.

Tvedten, I. and Hersoug, B. (ed) 1992. *Fishing for Development: Small-scale fisheries in Africa*. Nordiska Africainstitutet (The Scandanavian Institute of African Studies), Uppsala.

Weber, P. 1994. *Net Loss: Fish, jobs, and the marine environment*. World Watch Paper No. 120, USA.

Wise, J.P. 1991. *Federal Conservation and Management of Marine Fisheries in the United States*. Centre for Marine Conservation, Washington DC.

Sources of further information

Appropriate Technology Vol. 22, No 2. Sept 1995. IT Publications, London.

DEEP – Development Education Exchange Papers, Special Edition on Responsible Fisheries. September/October 1995. Office for External Relations, FAO.

The Ecologist: Overfishing Causes and Consequences. Vol. 25, No. 2/3 March/April, May/June 1995.

Fishing News International, EMAP Heighway, London, UK.

Maritime Anthropological Studies (MAST). Bi-annual journal. Het Spinhuis, Oudezijds, Achterburgwal 185, 1012 DK, Amsterdam, The Netherlands.

Samudra, News Magazine of ICSF. Published three times annually. ICSF, 27 College Rd, Madras 600 006, India.

World Fishing, Nexus Media Ltd, UK.

The Coalition for Fair Fisheries Agreements (CFFA), 65 Rue Gretry, B-1000 Brussels, Belgium. Tel: (+ 32 2) 2181538; fax: (+ 32 2) 2178305. CFFA is an association of European non-governmental organizations concerned about the developmental and environmental impacts of fisheries agreements negotiated between the European Union and the African, Caribbean, and Pacific states. CFFA is working for a fundamental change in the policy and practice on fisheries agreements between the EU and countries in the South (ACP States and others).

The International Centre for Living Aquatic Resources Management (ICLARM), MC PO Box 2631, 0718 Makati, Metro Manila, Philippines. Tel: + 63 2 8189283/817–5255. Fax: + 63 2 816 3183. Established in 1975 with the broad mandate to conduct and catalyse strategic research on all aspects of aquatic resource management, to publish and disseminate its findings, and recommendations, and to hold conferences to discuss current problems related to aquatic resources. Quartely publication, NAGA.

Mangrove Action Project, 4649 Sunnyside Ave. N. 321, Seattle WA 98103, USA. PO Box 1845, Port Angles, WA 98362–0279, USA. MAP is a coalition of individuals and organizations worldwide, working to protect and rehabilitate mangrove forests. Produces quarterly news bulletin.

The International Collective in Support of Fishworkers (ICSF). The main office is in Madras, India: 27 College Road, 600 006 Madras, India. Tel (+ 91 44) 8275303, Fax: (+ 91 44) 8254457. ICSF also maintains a liaison office in Brussels, Belgium: 65 Rue Gretry, B 1000, Brussels. ICSF is an international NGO, working on issues that concern fishworkers the world over. ICSF provides fishworkers (men, women and children) with a platform to make their voices heard at the international level so that the numerous problems they face on both land and sea may be taken into consideration by their governments and the international organizations.